THE OFFICIAL
LEICESTER CITY
QUIZ BOOK

THE OFFICIAL LEICESTER CITY QUIZ BOOK

**COMPILED BY
CHRIS COWLIN AND ADAM PEARSON**

FOREWORD BY TONY COTTEE

APEX PUBLISHING LTD

First published in 2008, Updated and reprinted in 2009 by
Apex Publishing Ltd
PO Box 7086, Clacton on Sea, Essex, CO15 5WN, England

www.apexpublishing.co.uk

**British Library Cataloguing-in-Publication Data
A catalogue record for this book
is available from the British Library**

ISBN 1-904444-86-5   978-1904444-86-2

Typeset in 10.5pt Chianti BdIt Win95BT

Cover Design: Siobham Smith

Printed in Great Britain by the MPG Books Group, Bodmin and King's Lynn

Author's Note:
Please can you contact ChrisCowlin@btconnect.com if you find any mistakes/errors in this book as I would like to put them right on any future reprints. I would also like to hear from Leicester City fans who have enjoyed the test! I can also be contacted via my website:
www.ChrisCowlin.com

FOREWORD

I left my hometown club, West Ham United, in October 1996 for what I was hoping would be an end of career, financially rewarding, swansong. By the time July the following year came around, I was desperately unhappy, homesick and missing English football. I wasn't too concerned, because I always felt that I would return to play for a few more years in England, the likely destinations being Orient, Southend or Colchester. Never in my wildest dreams, though, did I think that I would return to the Premiership, but when Steve Walford, an old teammate of mine and the now first team coach at Leicester City, called me to say that Martin O`Neill was interested in signing me, I was absolutely stunned. It was to be the start of three fantastic years of success for me and the club.

I signed in August 1997, a week after Robbie Savage had joined the club, and although I was made very welcome and became a part of the first team squad it took me a full six months to get fit and convince the manager that I was worthy of a starting place. Eventually Martin picked me, and I am proud to say that I was part of the team that won 1-0 at Old Trafford in January and scored the winning goal, my first ever at the Theatre of Dreams. I never looked back after that, and after establishing myself as a regular partner for Emile Heskey the goals flowed and the success came with it. I scored my 200th League goal at Spurs, played in Europe for the first time and played in the 1999 League Cup final, which we lost. I thought I was destined never to experience my first winners' medal, but the following year we beat Tranmere 2-1 and lifting the Cup that day was a memory that will stay with me forever.

My career lasted 20 years, but I can honestly say that my three-year spell at Leicester was my happiest time in the game. The joy came from the top, with Martin, Steve and John Robertson creating a fantastic team spirit and atmosphere around the place. The players revelled in it and, boy, did we have some fun! But, I look back with immense pride about two things. I was very lucky to have played with the likes of Lennon, Izzet, Walsh and many more outstanding players. We created a successful period for the club that will probably never be repeated. I also feel proud to have played for Leicester City FC, which is a wonderful club that has fantastic people working for it in all areas, at both the ground and training ground, and it is blessed with a very loyal and passionate group of supporters. Magical memories they were and, as I look back on the journey now, some seven years later, my feelings for the club haven't diminished; in fact, they have grown stronger. I am proud to say that "I was there!"

I am delighted to have been offered the chance to write this foreword for the Leicester City Quiz Book, because I have always been a football fan first and foremost and, like all fans, I pretend to know everything there is to know! We often used to have football quizzes on the way to away games when I was at the club, but sadly we didn't have a book like this to refer to, which meant there were too many arguments for my liking about who was right and who was wrong! Leicester City FC is a fantastic club and hopefully this book will answer all the questions and help you to look back on the glory days of old without the problems we had!

Enjoy the book!

Tony Cottee

INTRODUCTION
By Chris Cowlin

I would first of all like to thank Leicester City and footballing legend Tony Cottee for writing the foreword to this book. I have also been a great fan of Tony's and have watched him many times, so it was a true honour when he agreed to write a few words.

I am honoured to be able to donate £1 from each book sale to 'The Bobby Moore Fund for Cancer Research UK'. This charity raises money for research into bowel cancer in memory of footballer Bobby Moore.

I hope you enjoy this book. It was a true pleasure compiling it as well as working with Adam Pearson who has written quiz books on Southampton, England and the World Cup. I am sure that whatever section you choose to read first it will make you smile and the memories will come flooding back!

In closing, I would like to thank all my friends and family for encouraging me to complete this project.

Best wishes
Chris Cowlin

www.apexpublishing.co.uk

THE CLUB - RECORDS & HISTORY

1.   Can you name one of the three club nicknames?

2.   In what year was the club formed as Leicester Fosse?

3.   In what year did the club move to Filbert Street?

4.   Which player did Leicester City buy for a record
      £5 million from Wolves in July 2000?

5.   Against which team did Leicester record the biggest
      League win of their history in October 1928?

6.   Which player scored a record 44 goals in a season
      during 1956/1957?

7.   In March 2000, which team paid the club a record
      transfer fee for Emile Heskey?

8.   Against which London club did Leicester achieve their
      record attendance of 47,298 in February 1928?

9.   In which season did the club first play in European
      competition?

10.   In what year did Leicester City move to the Walkers
      Stadium?

MUZZY IZZET

11. In what year was Muzzy born - 1970, 1974 or 1978?

12. Which London team did Muzzy sign from to join Leicester City?

13. Against which team did Muzzy make his Leicester City debut on 30 March 1996 in a 2-0 home defeat?

14. In March 2001, Muzzy scored in a 2-0 home League win against Liverpool. Which other Leicester player scored?

15. In what position did Muzzy play during his career?

16. In October 1999, Muzzy scored a brace against which London side, in a 3-2 away League win?

17. Which manager signed Muzzy for Leicester in 1996?

18. For which International team did Muzzy win 8 full international caps during his career?

19. During the summer of 2004, Muzzy left the Foxes and joined which Midlands team?

20. What injury forced Muzzy out of the game during the summer of 2006?

MANAGERS

Match up the former Leicester City manager with the period he was in charge of the club

21.	David Pleat	1959 to 1968
22.	Brian Little	1971 to 1977
23.	Martin O'Neill	1946 to 1949
24.	Johnny Duncan	1932 to 1934
25.	Frank McLintock	1982 to 1986
26.	Peter Hodge	1991 to 1994
27.	Craig Levein	1977 to 1978
28.	Matt Gillies	1995 to 2000
29.	Gordon Milne	1987 to 1991
30.	Jimmy Bloomfield	2004 to 2006

MARTIN O'NEILL

31. In what year was Martin appointed as Leicester City manager?

32. Which award did Martin win in 2004 for his services to football?

33. Can you name the two years in which Leicester won the League Cup with Martin as manager?

34. In which season did Leicester gain promotion to the Premier League with Martin in charge at Filbert Street?

35. In which competition did Leicester compete for the first time in their history as a result of being League Cup winners whilst Martin was in charge of the club?

36. In August 2006, for which Midlands team was Martin appointed as manager?

37. How many full international caps did Martin gain as a Northern Ireland player - 44, 64 or 84?

38. For which team did Martin play between 1971 and 1981 under the management of Brian Clough?

39. Can you name one of Martin's two nicknames?

40. When Martin left Filbert Street in 2000, of which Scottish team did he become manager?

WHERE DID THEY GO? - 1

Match up the player with the club he moved to from Leicester

41.	Gareth Williams	Derby County
42.	Ian Walker	Southampton
43.	Dion Dublin	Kilmarnock
44.	Brian Deane	Wolverhampton Wanderers
45.	Andy Impey	Watford
46.	Spencer Prior	Bolton Wanderers
47.	Mark Draper	Celtic
48.	Mark Venus	West Ham United
49.	Russell Osman	Nottingham Forest
50.	Momo Sylla	Aston Villa

GORDON BANKS

51. In what year was Gordon born - 1927, 1937 or 1947?

52. In what position did Gordon play during his playing days?

53. Which team did Gordon sign from to join Leicester?

54. Following on from the previous question, in what year did that take place?

55. How many England caps did Gordon win for his country?

56. Which Foxes manager signed Gordon for Leicester for £7,000?

57. Which football award did Gordon win in 1972?

58. True or false: Gordon played in goal for England during their 1966 World Cup final success against West Germany?

59. In what year did Gordon make his England debut against Scotland, a 2-1 Wembley defeat for England?

60. By what nickname is Gordon most known?

THE CHAMPIONSHIP 2006/2007

61. Who scored twice when Leicester beat Ipswich 2-0 at Portman Road in February 2007?

62. Against which team did Leicester record their first League win of the season, winning 3-1 at home?

63. Who managed the Foxes during this season?

64. Which Canadian international forward scored a brace in the 3-2 home win against Southampton in October 2006?

65. Which Australian defender scored the only goal in the in the 1-0 win against Southend United in August 2006?

66. Which squad number did Andy Johnson wear during this season?

67. Which Yorkshire team did Leicester beat away from home in October 2006, with Danny Tiatto and Iain Hume scoring?

68. Which midfielder scored a last-minute winner against Wolves for Leicester to win 2-1 in December 2006?

69. Which Scottish midfielder left Leicester in the January transfer window to Watford?

70. Which player, whilst on loan to Leicester, scored on his debut in the 1-1 draw against Luton Town at the Walkers Stadium?

GARY LINEKER

71. In what year was Gary born - 1950, 1960 or 1970?

72. Gary made his Foxes debut on New Year's Day 1979 in a 2-0 home win, against which side?

73. What is Gary's middle name - Desmond, Winston or Rodney?

74. Can you name one of Gary's three nicknames?

75. How many League goals did Gary score for Leicester during his career - 65, 95 or 125?

76. Which Foxes manager handed Gary his debut for the club?

77. Against which team did Gary score his first Leicester City goal?

78. When Gary left Filbert Street in 1985, which top-flight team did he join?

79. For which Spanish team did Gary play between 1986 and 1989?

80. Gary played for England on 80 occasions, scoring how many goals, only one behind the record of Bobby Charlton?

LEAGUE CUP WINNERS 1964

81. Which team did Leicester beat 2-0 in round 2?

82. Which manager guided the club to this success?

83. True or false: this was the first time the club had won this cup?

84. Which cup final did Leicester play in the year before this one?

85. Against which London team did Leicester play in the semi-final of the competition?

86. Following on from the previous question, what was the aggregate score?

87. True or false: Leicester were runners-up in this competition a year later in 1965?

88. Can you name 7 of the starting 11 that won 3-2 in the final (2nd leg)?

89. Who scored in the cup final (1st leg) in the 1-1 away draw?

90. Leicester beat which team 4-3 on aggregate in the final?

EMILE HESKEY

91. *In what year was Emile born - 1978, 1982 or 1986?*

92. *Emile made his Leicester debut in March 1995 in a 2-0 defeat against which London team?*

93. *How many Premier League goals did Emile score for the Foxes during 1996/1997?*

94. *Against which East Anglian team did Emile score his first Leicester City career goal?*

95. *What was Emile's nickname whilst at Leicester City?*

96. *In February 1998, against which London team did Emile score a brace in a 2-0 home win?*

97. *When Emile left Leicester in 2000, which top-flight team did he join?*

98. *In August 1999, Emile scored a brace against Middlesbrough in a 3-0 away win. Which Foxes striker scored the other goal?*

99. *Which Foxes manager gave Emile his Leicester debut?*

100. *Which team did Emile sign for from Birmingham City in July 2006?*

LEICESTER v. NOTTINGHAM FOREST

101. In what year did Leicester last play Nottingham Forest as Leicester Fosse in the League?

102. On 28 February 1981, Leicester City and Nottingham Forest played out a 1-1 League Division One draw at Filbert Street. Who scored the goal for Leicester that afternoon?

103. The Foxes' visit to the city ground on 4 December 1983 was a first for the team. Why?

104. On 5 May 1984, Leicester City achieved a long-awaited League win over Nottingham Forest at Filbert Street. Who scored Leicester's decisive second goal in that afternoon's 2-1 victory?

105. In which 1990s season did Leicester City first finish above Nottingham Forest in the Premier League?

106. Who scored on his Leicester City debut against Nottingham Forest in the League Cup second leg 2-1 defeat on November 30th 1988?

107. In season 1971/1972, Leicester beat Nottingham Forest twice by the same scoreline in the League, both home and away. What was the score?

108. What was the final score in the 6-goal Division One thriller between the two teams on 4 May 1968 at Filbert Street?

109. On 25 August 1962, Leicester beat Forest 2-1 at Filbert Street with a brace from a player with a surname that sounds like he might now be the owner of a nightclub. Name him.

110. Which player did City sign from Forest in 1989, who only made a handful of appearances for the club that season?

ALAN YOUNG

111. Against which club did Alan make a two-goal scoring debut on 18 August 1979?

112. How many League and Cup goals did Alan score in total in his first season with Leicester City?

113. From which club did Leicester sign Alan?

114. Against which Midlands club did Alan score his first Division One goal for Leicester on 25 October 1980?

115. Against which club was Alan required to play in goal due to an injury to Mark Wallington in the FA Cup on 6 March 1982?

116. Alan was one of two Leicester City players dismissed in the League game against Brighton on 20 April 1981. Which other player was sent off in that match?

117. Against which club did Alan score his last two goals for Leicester City on 27 March 1982?

118. In what town was Alan born?

119. How many League and Cup goals did Alan score for Leicester City - 29, 39 or 49?

120. To which club did Alan move in 1982?

CITY TRANSFERS

121. During July 2007, how much did Leicetser pay for Stephen Clemence?

122. Gareth McAuley signed for Leicester from which club in June 2006?

123. Jason Wilcox left the club and signed for which club in January 2006?

124. Scot Gemmill signed from which club in August 2005?

125. How much did Leicester pay Tranmere Rovers for Iain Hume in August 2005?

126. Leeds United paid £1 million for which Foxes player in July 1990?

127. David Oldfield left Leicester for £150,000 and joined which club?

128. From which French team did Leicester sign Peggy Arphexad?

129. From which club was Robbie Savage signed in August 1997?

130. How much did Leicester receive for Gary Mills when he signed for Notts County in September 1994?

1970s

131. The 1970s began for Leicester City with a 1-0 FA Cup victory at Filbert Street against which north-east club?

132. When Leicester won the Division Two championship in 1971, who were runners-up?

133. How many managers did Leicester City employ during the 1970s?

134. What honour did Leicester City win in August 1971?

135. Who beat Leicester City in the FA Cup 3rd/4th place play-off in 1974?

136. In what month and year did Peter Shilton leave Leicester City?

137. In the dismal relegation season of 1977/1978, who did Leicester beat on the last day of the season?

138. Who was Leicester's top goalscorer in 1976/1977?

139. Against which club did Mark Wallington make his clean-sheet Leicester first-team debut on 11 March 1972?

140. How many seasons of the 1970s did Leicester spend in Division One?

NATIONALITIES - 1

Match up the player with his nationality

141.	Rab Douglas	Ghanaian
142.	Andy King	Australian
143.	Jimmy Nielsen	Jamaican
144.	Tony Cottee	Scottish
145.	Bruno N'Gotty	Danish
146.	Elvis Hammond	English
147.	Paul Henderson	Welsh
148.	Ricky Sappleton	Canadian
149.	Iain Hume	English
150.	Emile Heskey	French

MANAGERS OF THE FOXES

151. Can you name the first ever manager of the club, who was in charge between 1884 and 1892?

152. Which London club did David Pleat manage before the Foxes?

153. Which manager handed a debut to David Nish?

154. Which player was Jimmy Bloomfield's first purchase in 1971?

155. In what year did Brian Little join the club as manager?

156. When David Pleat left the club in January 1991, which manager took over until May of that year?

157. Which manager was in charge of the Foxes between December 1968 and June 1971?

158. Which manager handed a debut to Garry Parker when he was signed from Aston Villa in 1994?

159. Which manager was in charge of the Foxes between June 1955 and October 1958?

160. Which manager took over at the club in May 2007 only to leave during August 2007, having only been in charge for three League games and one League Cup game?

POT LUCK - 1

161. Which player became Leicester's first £1 million signing during July 1994?

162. In what position did Bob Lee play?

163. When Leonard Glover made his debut in November 1967 at Filbert Street, who were Leicester playing?

164. Which goalkeeper made his debut in September 1959 having signed for Leicester from Chesterfield?

165. How many League goals did Ian Banks score in his Foxes career - 10, 14 or 18?

166. Which player scored on his debut in November 1981 at Filbert Street, but only made four appearances for the club?

167. Which player made a scoring debut against Birmingham City at home during April 1961?

168. In what position did Bob Nicky Platnauer play?

169. How many League appearances did Norman Plummer make for the Foxes - 66, 76 or 86?

170. Who scored a hat-trick against Derby County in the 3-3 home draw in April 1994?

BOBBY SMITH

171. From which club did Leicester sign Bobby?

172. In what year did Bobby score his first Leicester City League goal?

173. In what year did Bobby score his last League goal for Leicester City?

174. Against which club did Bobby score an FA Cup winner on 26 January 1985?

175. In which season was Bobby Leicester's second top goalscorer?

176. Bobby scored only one goal during which season in the first League game against Everton at Filbert Street?

177. In which two consecutive seasons of his Leicester City career did Bobby not play any first team football for the club?

178. Against which club did Bobby score an FA Cup winner for Leicester on 4 January 1992, his last competitive goal for the club?

179. In which season did Bobby make his final appearance for Leicester City?

180. Which club did Bobby join when he left the Foxes?

LEICESTER v. ASTON VILLA

181.   Who scored Leicester's first ever Premiership goal against Aston Villa?

182.   In what year did Leicester and Aston Villa first meet in the League - 1898, 1908 or 1918?

183.   Which Aston Villa striker did Leicester sign in 2000?

184.   Which striker left the club to join Aston Villa in 1996?

185.   Who scored Leicester's first goal in the 2-1 FA Cup 4th round victory over Aston Villa on 27 January 2001?

186.   In the 1996/1997 season, Leicester achieved a Premiership double over Aston Villa, winning 3-1 at Villa Park and 1-0 at Filbert Street. Which player scored against Villa in both matches?

187.   On 4 April 1970, Leicester City beat Aston Villa 1-0, helping to seal Villa's fate that season. What happened to Villa at the end of the 1969/1970 season?

188.   On 4 April 1981, Leicester lost 4-2 at home to Aston Villa. Who scored Leicester's two goals that day (one from the penalty spot)?

189.   Who scored Leicester's first goal of the season in the Premiership opener against Aston Villa at Filbert Street on 9 August 1997?

190.   In season 1998/1999, the Foxes and Aston Villa played out two draws in the Premiership. Which Leicester player scored in both meetings?

PREMIER LEAGUE 1997/1998

191. Which manager was in charge of Leicester durng this season?

192. Leicester lost 5-3 away to which Lancashire club in February 1998?

193. Which visiting team attracted the biggest attendance of 21,669 during the 1997/1998 season at Filbert Street?

194. During September 1997, Leicester beat Spurs 3-0 at home. Can you name the three goalscorers?

195. What was the score when Leicester met Derby County at the Baseball Ground?

196. In January 1998, Leicester beat Manchester United 1-0 at Old Trafford, can you name the scorer?

197. When Leicester played Arsenal at home the score was 3-3. Can you name the Foxes' goalscorers?

198. Following on from the previous question, can you name the Gunners' hat-trick hero in the game?

199. In what position did Leicester finish in the Premier League?

200. Who scored the only goal in the 1-0 home win in May 1998 against Barnsley?

DAVID NISH

201. In what year did David make his goalscoring debut for Leicester City?

202. In which season did David score a total of 10 League and Cup goals for Leicester City?

203. What FA Cup record did David set in 1969?

204. In what town was David born?

205. What was the only League honour that Leicester won whilst David was a player?

206. Against which London club did David score his last two goals for Leicester City on 11 March 1972?

207. How many appearances did David make for Leicester City - 255, 266 or 277?

208. What club did David join when he left Leicester City?

209. What transfer fee did Leicester receive when David left the club in 1972?

210. In 1988 David accepted a coaching position at which club?

ALAN BIRCHENALL

211. Where in London was Alan born?

212. From which club did Leicester City sign Alan?

213. In what year was Alan born?

214. In what year did Alan make his Leicester City debut?

215. Against which London club did Alan score his first Leicester City goal?

216. Against which high-flying Division One club did Alan score both of Leicester's goals in a 2-0 win on 10 February 1973 at Filbert Street?

217. In 1975 it took Leicester three goes to achieve a result in their FA Cup 5th round tie. Alan scored the only goal (his last for Leicester) in the three matches, but who did he score against?

218. In what year did Alan leave Leicester City?

219. How many appearances did Alan make for Leicester City - 176, 186 or 196?

220. Which club did Alan join when he left Leicester City?

FRANK WORTHINGTON

221. Frank was born in Halifax, in which year?

222. In what year did Frank make his City debut on 23 August - 1970, 1971 or 1972?

223. Following on from the previous question, Frank made a scoring debut, against which club?

224. How many League appearances did Frank make for the club during his career?

225. In what position did Frank play for the Foxes?

226. How many League goals did Frank score for Leicester during his career - 62, 72 or 82?

227. Which Foxes manager signed Frank for the club?

228. What is Frank's middle name?

229. From which club did Leicester sign Frank?

230. Between 1985 and 1987, which team did Frank manage?

IN WHAT YEAR?

Match up the year with the event

231. Frank McLintock was appointed manager   1949

232. Leonard Glover made his City debut   1984
against Arsenal at home

233. Kevin Poole was born   1970

234. Ian Andrews made his City debut   1987
against Wolves

235. James Walsh was born   1980

236. Norman Bullock took over as manager   1977

237. Dennis Rofe left for Chelsea   1960

238. Richard Smith was born   1963

239. George Meek joined from Leeds United   1967

240. Mike Newell scored on his City debut
against Oldham Athletic   1930

WHERE DID THEY COME FROM?

Match up the player with the club from which he was signed for Leicester City

241.	Phil Gee	Wolves
242.	Stephen Clemence	Aston Villa
243.	Pat Byrne	Sheffield United
244.	Arthur Maw	Birmingham City
245.	Franz Carr	Arsenal
246.	Carl Cort	Birmingham City
247.	Bob Hazell	Notts County
248.	DJ Campbell	Derby County
249.	Allan Evans	Shelbourne
250.	Jon Sammels	Queens Park Rangers

LEICESTER IN THE FA CUP

251. Against which non-League club, in 1975, did Leicester come back from 2-0 down to win 3-2?

252. Who scored Leicester City's goal in the 1949 FA Cup final against Wolverhampton Wanderers?

253. Whom did Leicester beat in the 1949 FA Cup semi-final at Highbury?

254. It took three attempts for Leicester to beat which club in the 1961 FA Cup semi-final?

255. Who scored Leicester City's goal against Manchester United in the 1963 FA Cup final?

256. Whom did Leicester City knock out of the 1969 FA Cup in the 5th round?

257. In 2000, whom did Leicester City knock out of the FA Cup after two 0-0 draws and a penalty shootout?

258. Which Leicester City player has made the most appearances for the Foxes in the FA Cup?

259. Who scored a goal for Leicester in both the semi-final and semi-final replay of 1954 against Preston North End?

260. Who captained Leicester in the 1949 FA Cup final?

1990s

261. Which south coast club were beaten by Leicester on the first day of the 1990s?

262. The Foxes had to win the final match of the 1990/1991 season to avoid relegation to Division Three. Whom did Leicester beat 1-0 that day?

263. What was the final score in the Division Two play-off semi-final 2nd leg when Leicester City played Cambridge United on 13 May 1992?

264. Which club did Leicester knock out in the Division Two play-off semi-finals of 1992/1993?

265. Who was Leicester City's top goalscorer in all competitions in the promotion season of 1993/1994?

266. Who was Leicester's top goalscorer in 1994/1995, their first ever season in the Premiership?

267. On 17 September 1994, Leicester achieved their first win in the Premiership. Which London club were the Foxes' victims that day?

268. Who was Leicester's top goalscorer in the 1996/1997 Premiership campaign?

269. Whose first goal for Leicester was a long-range 'screamer' and the winning goal against Southampton at the Dell on 13 December 1997?

270. Who scored Leicester City's last League goal of the 1990s in a 2-1 defeat to Newcastle United at Filbert Street on 28 December 1999?

UNUSUAL RESULTS

Match up the fixture with the final score

271. *v. Manchester United (Home)*   **4-5**
January 1999, Premiership

272. *v. Fulham (Home)*   **3-5**
September 1979, Division Two

273. *v. Leeds United (Home)*   **6-3**
November 1989, Division Two

274. *v. West Ham United (Home)*   **6-4**
August 1966, Division One

275. *v. Watford (Home)*   **3-3**
December 1993, Division One

276. *v. Notts County (Home)*   **2-6**
September 1956, Division Two

277. *v. Fulham (Away)*   **5-3**
September 1952, Division Two

278. *v. Leyton Orient (Home)*   **4-4**
February 1979, Division Two

279. *v. Southampton (Away)*   **4-3**
April 1950, Division Two

280. *v. Newcastle United (Away)*   **5-4**
January 1990, Division Two

DIVISION TWO CHAMPIONS 1980

281. Who captained Leicester to the 1979/1980 Division Two championship?

282. Against which London club did Leicester achieve their biggest win in the championship campaign of 1979/1980?

283. Who scored the goal that sealed the championship for Leicester on the last day of the 1979/1980 season at Orient?

284. How many goals did Gary Lineker score during the 1979/1980 season?

285. Leicester achieved a 7-game unbeaten run at the end of the 1979/1980 season to seal the Division Two title. Against which London club did they begin the run at Filbert Street with a 1-0 win on 5 April 1980?

286. Against which club did Leicester record their lowest home attendance of the 1979/1980 season?

287. Which two clubs were promoted with Leicester City in 1980?

288. Who was the last team to beat Leicester in the 1979/1980 season?

289. Against which club did Gary Lineker score both of Leicester's goals in a 2-1 win at Filbert Street on 27 October 1979?

290. Three Leicester players played in all 42 League games in 1979/1980. Name them.

ALLY MAUCHLEN

291. In what year was Ally born?

292. In which Scottish county was Ally born?

293. From which Scottish club did Leicester sign Ally?

294. In what year did Ally make his Leicester City debut?

295. Against which club did Ally score his first goal for Leicester in a 2-2 draw on 1 February 1986?

296. In which season did Ally score his highest season goal tally for Leicester?

297. Against which club did Ally score his last goal for Leicester on 26 December 1991?

298. Which manager was in charge when Ally played his last game for Leicester?

299. How many League and Cup appearances did Ally make for Leicester - 238, 248 or 258?

300. How many League and Cup goals did Ally score for Leicester - 9, 11 or 13?

FRANK McLINTOCK

301.   Frank was born in what year - 1933, 1936 or 1939?

302.   Which nationality is Frank - English, Scottish or Irish?

303.   Frank made his Leicester City debut in September 1959, against which team?

304.   True or false: Frank made 178 League appearances for the Foxes during his career?

305.   In what year did Frank win the Football Writers' Association Footballer of the Year award, the same year that he also won the League and FA Cup double with Arsenal?

306.   How many League goals did Frank score for Leicester during his career - 15, 25 or 35?

307.   Frank left Leicetser for Arsenal in which year?

308.   Which award did Frank receive from the Queen during 1972?

309.   Which manager signed Frank for the Foxes?

310.   For which London team did Frank leave Arsenal in 1973?

JON SAMMELS

311. In what town was Jon born?

312. From which club did Leicester sign Jon?

313. How much did Leicester pay to sign Jon?

314. Against which club did Jon make his Leicester debut on 7 August 1971?

315. Against which club did Jon score his first goal for Leicester?

316. On 13 September 1975, Jon scored two of Leicester's goals in a 3-3 draw against which London club?

317. Against which Midlands club did Jon score his last goal for Leicester from the penalty spot on 15 October 1977?

318. How many appearances did Jon make for Leicester City - 277, 287 or 297?

319. How many goals did Jon score for Leicester - 9, 19 or 29?

320. Which American club did Jon join when he left Leicester in 1978?

ALAN SMITH

321. In what year was Alan born in Birmingham?

322. Which manager signed Alan for Leicester, his final signing at the club before Gordon Milne took over?

323. How many League appearances did Alan make for the Foxes during his career?

324. Alan made his Leicester debut against which London club during August 1982?

325. How many goals did Alan score for England during his 13 caps?

326. How many League goals did Alan score during his Leicester career - 76, 78 or 80?

327. At which non-League club did Alan start his football career?

328. Against which country did Alan make his full England debut?

329. Alan left Leicester in 1987 and joined which London club?

330. In what position did Alan play for the Foxes?

LEICESTER V. WEST BROM

331. In what year did Leicester Fosse and West Bromwich Albion first meet in the Football League?

332. Who scored the winning goal for Leicester in the FA Cup semi-final of 1969 against West Bromwich Albion?

333. In the 1972/1973 season, West Bromwich Albion finished bottom of Division One. Leicester helped them on their way down by beating them at Filbert Street. What was the final score of what turned out to be the Foxes' biggest win of the season?

334. The last time that Leicester and West Bromwich Albion met at Filbert Street was in the new Division One on 9 April 1996. Leicester lost 2-1, but who scored the Foxes' goal?

335. On 8 September 1993, City played Albion in the Anglo Italian Cup. What was the final score of the Filbert Street match?

336. In the 1985/1986 season, both Division One games between Leicester City and West Bromwich Albion ended in the same drawn scoreline. What was it?

337. Whom did Leicester sign from West Bromwich Albion for the 1983/1984 season?

338. Who scored his last goal for Leicester City in his penultimate game for the club in a 4-2 victory over West Bromwich Albion on 30 September 1964?

339. Signed from Peterborough United in 1965, he scored in both League meetings against West Bromwich Albion during the 1965/1966 season. Leicester won the home game 2-1 but lost the away game 5-1. Who was he?

340. In the 1954/1955 season, Leicester's biggest League win was at home to West Bromwich Albion, when they won 6-3 at Filbert Street. Earlier in the season City had lost 6-4 to the Albion at the Hawthornes. Which Leicester player scored four goals during those two games?

JAMES (JIMMY) WALSH

341.   In what city was Jimmy born?

342.   From which club did Leicester sign Jimmy?

343.   In what year did Jimmy make his Leicester debut?

344.   In 1961, Jimmy scored Leicester's first ever goal in European competition. Which Irish club conceded that goal?

345.   Jimmy was one of the first professional footballers to do what: have an agent, wear contact lenses, write a newspaper column or own a sports car?

346.   On 22 February 1958, Jimmy scored four of the Foxes' eight goals against which club?

347.   In which season did Jimmy become Leicester's captain?

348.   In which season was Jimmy Leicester's top goalscorer, with 29 goals?

349.   Against which club did Jimmy score his last goal for Leicester?

350.   In what year did Jimmy leave Leicester to join Rugby Town?

PREMIER LEAGUE 2003/2004

351. Who scored Leicester's last Premiership goal of the 2003/2004 season at Highbury against Arsenal?

352. Who scored Leicester's winning goal in the 1-0 win against Birmingham City at St Andrews?

353. On 6 December 2003, Leicester drew 1-1 against Arsenal at the Walkers Stadium. Who scored Leicester's last-minute equaliser?

354. On 9 November 2003, Leicester travelled to the City of

    Manchester Stadium and gained a memorable victory. What was the final score of that match?

355. On 15 September 2003, Leicester chalked up their biggest victory of the 2003/2004 season. Whom did they beat 4-0?

356. On 22 February 2004, Leicester and Tottenham played out an eight-goal thriller at White Hart Lane. What was the final score of that match?

357. On 31 January 2004, Leicester crashed to their biggest defeat of the 2003/2004 season. Which Midlands club inflicted that 5-0 trouncing at the Walkers Stadium?

358. Whom did Leicester knock out of the Carling Cup second round on 23 September 2003?

359. Who knocked Leicester out of the 2004 FA Cup after a third round replay?

360. Which two clubs finished below the Foxes in the 2003/2004 Premiership table?

STEVE LYNEX

361. Where was Steve born?

362. From what club did Leicester City sign Steve?

363. In what year did Steve join Leicester City?

364. How many goals did Steve score in the 12 games he played in his first season for Leicester?

365. Against which London club did Steve score both his first and his last Leicester goals?

366. Of the 10 goals that Steve scored for Leicester in the 1981/1982 season, how many of them were from the penalty spot?

367. Against which club did Steve score a hat-trick, along with Gary Lineker, in a Division Two game at Filbert Street on 11 September 1982?

368. Steve scored his first FA Cup goal for Leicester in an FA Cup third round match against Burton Albion, in what year?

369. In which season was Steve the second top goalscorer to Gary Lineker for the Foxes?

370. Whom did Steve join when he left Leicester City in 1987?

STEVE WALSH

371. From what club did Leicester sign Steve?

372. What fee did Leicester pay to sign Steve?

373. Which manager did Steve follow to join Leicester?

374. Early in his Leicester City career, Steve served a lengthy suspension after an incident with which Shrewsbury Town player?

375. Against which Midlands club did Steve score his first Leicester City goal?

376. In which season was Steve Leicester's top goalscorer?

377. Against which Premiership club did Steve score his last goal for Leicester City?

378. How many appearances did Steve make for Leicester - 428, 438 or 448?

379. Which club did Steve join when he left Leicester?

380. Which other player joined the same club as Steve when he left Leicester at the same time?

PREMIER LEAGUE 1998/1999

381. To which club did Leicester travel on the opening day of the season, 15 August 1998, to gain a creditable 2-2 draw?

382. Who was Leicester's first-choice goalkeeper during the 1998/1999 season?

383. Who were Leicester's second round victims on their route to Wembley in the League Cup of 1998/1999?

384. Who was Leicester's top goalscorer in 1998/1999?

385. Who was the only Leicester player to start every Premiership game of the 1998/1999 season?

386. Who knocked Leicester out of the FA Cup in round four of the 1998/1999 season?

387. Who scored all of Leicester's three semi-final goals in the League Cup run of 1998/1999?

388. Which club did Leicester beat 1-0 both home and away in 1998/1999?

389. Against which club did Leicester record their lowest home Premiership attendance (17,725) in 1998/1999?

390. In what position did Leicester finish in the Premiership table of 1998/1999?

CAPS FOR MY COUNTRY

Match up the player with the number of caps achieved

391.	Tony Cottee (England)	80
392.	Gordon Banks (England)	57
393.	Peter Shilton (England)	7
394.	Frank Worthington (England)	18
395.	Gary McAllister (Scotland)	73
396.	Derek Dougan (Northern Ireland)	8
397.	Muzzy Izzet (Turkey)	43
398.	Gary Lineker (England)	7
399.	Matt Elliott (Scotland)	125
400.	Steve Whitworth (England)	8

MATT GILLIES

401.   Where was Matt born?

402.   What is Matt's middle name?

403.   From what club did Leicester sign Matt?

404.   In what position did Matt play for Leicester City?

405.   In what year did Matt become Leicester manager (as caretaker)?

406.   In what year did Matt make his Leicester debut?

407.   Which player did Matt sign for a then record transfer fee of £150,000?

408.   Which Leicester manager brought Matt to Filbert Street?

409.   In which season did Matt play his last game for Leicester?

410.   For how many seasons was Matt Leicester's manager?

DIVISION ONE PLAY-OFF WINNERS 1994

411. In what position did Leicester finish in Division One to qualify for the play-offs?

412. Which club did Leicester's final opponents, Derby County, knock out of the 1994 Division One play-off semi-final?

413. Which Leicester City player had formerly played for the opposition in the 1994 Division One play-off final?

414. Whom did Leicester City beat in the Division One play-off semi-final of 1994?

415. What was the half-time score in the 1994 play-off final between Leicester and Derby?

416. Who scored both of Leicester's goals in the 1994 play-off final?

417. Which two players scored Leicester City's two semi-final goals in the 1994 Division One play-offs?

418. What was the attendance of the 1994 play-off final at Wembley Stadium - 73,802, 78,802 or 83,802?

419. Leicester's play-off final win against Derby County in 1994 ended the worst Wembley record for any club. On how many previous occasions had the Foxes departed from the twin towers as losers?

420. Which Leicester player scored four goals against Derby in the two League meetings between the Foxes and the Rams during 1993/1994?

POSITIONS IN THE LEAGUE - 1

*Match up the season with the position
in which Leicester finished*

421.	2006/2007	The Championship	9th
422.	2004/2005	The Championship	10th
423.	2002/2003	Division One	15th
424.	2000/2001	Premier League	21st
425.	1998/1999	Premier League	2nd
426.	1996/1997	Premier League	15th
427.	1994/1995	Premier League	22nd
428.	1992/1993	Division One	19th
429.	1990/1991	Division Two	13th
430.	1988/1989	Division Two	6th

POT LUCK - 2

431. How many League goals did Paul Kitson score during his Leicester career?

432. In what country was David Oldfield born?

433. From which team was Alan Parris signed to join the Foxes during July 1988?

434. In what position did Garry Parker play for Leicester during his playing days?

435. Against which club did Lee Philpott make his Foxes debut during November 1992?

436. Which 'Paul' scored on his debut at home against Huddersfield Town in May 1988 after coming on as a substitute?

437. How many League goals did Paul Ramsey score during his Leicester career?

438. Steve Thompson left Filbert Street in February 1995 and joined which team?

439. Goalkeeper Mark Wallington made how many appearances (in all competitions) for the club - 400, 460 or 520?

440. Kevin Campbell made 11 League appearances at City whilst on loan during 1989/1990. How many goals did he score?

LEAGUE GOALSCORERS - 1

*Match up the player with the total number of
League goals scored for Leicester City*

441.	Darren Eadie	57
442.	Marc North	4
443.	Iwan Roberts	2
444.	Dean Smith	41
445.	Mark Robins	38
446.	Peter Welsh	1
447.	Bobby Svarc	9
448.	Muzzy Izzet	12
449.	Steve Lynex	9
450.	Steve Guppy	2

1960s

451. Who was manager of Leicester City at the start of the 1960s?

452. Who scored Leicester's first goal of the 1960s?

453. Who was Leicester's top scorer during the 1959/1960 season?

454. At the end of which 1960s season were Leicester relegated to Division Two?

455. In which 1960s season did Leicester finish fourth in Division One (their highest position of the decade)?

456. In the 1960s, Leicester set a record for consecutive League and FA Cup wins. What was the record - 9, 10 or 11?

457. Whom did Leicester knock out of the 1965 League Cup semi-final?

458. Which Leicester legend made his debut against Everton on 4 May 1966?

459. Who scored Leicester's last Division One goal of the 1960s?

460. Who scored Leicester's last goal of the 1960s?

WHO SCORED ...?

461.   In the League Cup 1-0 win against Accrington, 1st round, during August 2007?

462.   In the Premier League in the 1-0 win during April 1995 against Norwich City?

463.   Twice in the 4-0 home win against Leeds United during September 2003?

464.   A last-minute goal in the 1-1 League draw against Arsenal in December 2003?

465.   The first goal of Leicester's League season during 1998/1999?

466.   The only goal in the 1-0 League Cup final win in 1997?

467.   Two goals in the 3-1 home League win against Tottenham Hotspur in September 1994?

468.   Leicester's first goal in the 3-2 League Cup final win (2nd leg) in 1964?

469.   Arsenal's three goals (hat-trick) in the 3-3 Premier League win at Filbert Street during August 1997?

470.   The UEFA Cup 1st round, 1st leg goal in the 2-1 away defeat against Athletico Madrid during September 1997?

PETER SHILTON

471. Where in the country was Peter born in 1949?

472. In what year was Peter handed his Leicester debut?

473. Following on from the previous question, whom were Leicester playing in this match?

474. Which honour did Peter receive from the Queen in 1986?

475. How many League appearances did Peter make for the Foxes - 186, 286 or 386?

476. When Peter left Leicester in November 1974, which club did he join?

477. For which team did Peter play between 1977 and 1982?

478. How many clean sheets did Peter keep during the 1970/1971 season - 17, 20 or 23?

479. True or false: Peter scored for Leicester during his career?

480. How many England caps does Peter have to his name - 125, 130 or 135?

WHO AM I?

481. I was a striker and became the youngest ever League appearance maker for the club. I scored on my debut at home on New Year's Day 1979.

482. I was born in Kilrea, near Coleraine in March 1952. I was a midfielder and ended my playing days at Notts County. I became manager of Wycombe Wanderers in 1990.

483. I was born in 1938 and was an inside forward for the Foxes. I signed from Hibs in January 1962 and left the club in September 1970 for Aston Villa.

484. I was born in 1969, and I was the first captain to raise a trophy at Wembley in the 1994 play-off final?

485. I spent a loan spell at the club from Spurs and made my debut during October 1990 against Ipswich Town.

486. I was born in 1962, played as a midfielder, scored 13 League goals for City during my career and gained 14 Northern Ireland caps.

487. I was a midfielder, and I scored on my debut against Oxford in 1990 after coming on as a subsitute.

488. I was a left back, I made my debut against Aston Villa in March 1986 away from home and signed from Hartlepool United. I left for Wolves in 1988.

489. I was a striker and made my debut in September 1985, scoring against Birmingham City away from home.

490. I was a centre back, born in London in 1946. I made 32 (1) League appearances and 2 FA Cup appearances for City. My debut was against Wolves in October 1977.

GARY MILLS

491. Where was Gary born?

492. From which club did Leicester sign Gary?

493. Against which club did Gary score his first goal for Leicester on 25 November 1989?

494. Which manager signed Gary for Leicester?

495. In 1991, Gary captained Leicester to within a goal of relegation from Division Two. Whom did Leicester beat on the last day of the season to stay up?

496. In which season did Gary score his highest total of League and Cup goals for Leicester?

497. Which new manager, in 1991, retained Gary as Leicester captain?

498. How many appearances, in all competitions, did Gary make for Leicester in 1991/1992 - 50, 60 or 70?

499. At which club did Gary begin his professional football career?

500. Which club did Gary join when he left Leicester in 1994?

COLIN APPLETON

501. Leicester signed Colin from his hometown club. Which club was that?

502. In what year did Colin make his Leicester City debut?

503. In what year did Colin score his first goal for Leicester?

504. In which season did Colin play in every one of Leicester's League and Cup matches, scoring five goals for the club?

505. In the 1960/1961 season, Colin scored Leicester's opening goal of the campaign against which club?

506. For which club did Colin score his only European competition goal?

507. Which manager made Colin captain of Leicester City?

508. In which season did Colin score his highest total of goals in a campaign for Leicester City (10 goals)?

509. In what year did Colin leave Leicester?

510. Which club did Colin join when he left the Foxes?

LEICESTER V. COVENTRY CITY

511.   In what year did Leicester City and Coventry City first meet in the League - 1919, 1920 or 1921?

512.   Who scored Leicester's first two Premiership goals against Coventry City in a 2-2 draw at Filbert Street on 3 October 1994?

513.   Leicester achieved their first Premiership victory against Coventry City on 29 November 1997 at Highfield Road. What was the final score of that game?

514.   On 17 February 2007, Leicester beat Coventry 3-0 at the Walkers Stadium in the Coca-Cola Championship. Who scored two goals for the Foxes that day?

515.   On 11 August 1999, Leicester beat Coventry 1-0 at Filbert Street in the Premiership. Who scored the Foxes' winner?

516.   On 1 December 1964, Leicester achieved their biggest victory over Coventry, in a League Cup tie at Highfield Road. What was the final score of that game?

517.   On 23 December 1984, Leicester thrashed Coventry at Filbert Street in Division One. What was the final score of that game?

518.   On 12 March 1977, Leicester City beat Coventry City 3-1 at Filbert Street. Brian Alderson and Steve Earle scored the first two goals for the Foxes, but who scored the third?

519.   Which player did Leicester City sign from Coventry City in 1982?

520.   Who was the Glaswegian that left Leicester to sign for Coventry in 1982?

RUSSELL OSMAN

521. In what year was Russell born in Derbyshire - 1957, 1959 or 1961?

522. In what year did Russell join Leicester?

523. Against which team did Russell make his Foxes debut?

524. How many League goals did Russell score in all competitions during his Leicester career?

525. Which Cup did Russell win with Ipswich Town in 1981?

526. Which Leicester manager signed Russell for Leicester, costing £240,000?

527. True or false: Russell played 108 League games for the club during his football career?

528. In what position did Russell play during his playing days?

529. Of which team was Russell appointed player/coach during April 1995?

530. When Russell left Leicester, which team did he join during June 1988?

PREMIER LEAGUE 1999/2000

531. Which player scored a penalty in Leicester's first win of the season, 1-0 at home against Coventry City?

532. Which manager was in charge at the club during this season?

533. True or false: Leicester finished 8th in the Premier League?

534. How many games did Leicester win during their 38 League matches - 16, 20 or 24?

535. Which two players scored in the 2-0 away win against Liverpool in May 2000?

536. Which player scored a brace in the 3-0 away win against Middlesbrough in August 1999?

537. True or false: Leicester beat Bradford City 5-0 at home during May 2000?

538. Which player finished as top League goalscorer with 13 goals?

539. On 3 October 1999, Leicester beat Spurs 3-2 at White Hart Lane, but which player scored a brace for the Foxes?

540. Which former Aston Villa and Liverpool striker signed for the club in February 2000?

LEAGUE CUP WINNERS 1964

541. Can you name the five clubs that Leicester knocked out of the 1963/1964 League Cup on their way to the final?

542. How many goals did Leicester score throughout the 1963/1964 League Cup competition?

543. Who scored Leicester's goal in the drawn League Cup final first leg at the Victoria Ground on 15 April 1964 and their second goal of the return match at Filbert Street a week later?

544. Who scored Leicester's opening goal of the League Cup final second leg at Filbert Street on 22 April 1964?

545. How many players that played in the League Cup final first leg of 1964 were left out of the team in the return match at Filbert Street?

546. Name the Scottish international who scored in both legs of the League Cup semi-final of 1964 for Leicester but missed out on playing in the final against Stoke City.

547. How many goals did Leicester concede throughout the whole of the 1963/1964 League Cup competition?

548. When Leicester won their opening game of the 1963/1964 tournament this was the start of a long unbeaten run in the competition. For how many matches did the Foxes remain unbeaten in the League Cup until 1965?

549. Who is missing from this Leicester line-up for the League Cup final second leg of 1964 - Banks, Norman, Cross, King, Appleton, Riley, Gibson, Keyworth, Sweenie and Stringfellow?

550. Which player in Leicester's 1964 League Cup final team later played for opponents Stoke City in the League Cup final of 1972?

TOP LEAGUE GOALSCORER IN A SEASON

Match up the season with Leicester's top goalscorer

551.	2006/2007	Tony Cottee (13)
552.	2005/2006	Ade Akinbiyi (9)
553.	2004/2005	Brian Deane (6)
554.	2003/2004	Emile Heskey (10)
555.	2002/2003	Tony Cottee (10)
556.	2001/2002	David Connolly (13)
557.	2000/2001	Iain Hume (9)
558.	1999/2000	Les Ferdinand (12)
559.	1998/1999	Paul Dickov (17)
560.	1997/1998	Iain Hume (13)

PREMIER LEAGUE 1994/1995

561. Who scored Leicester's first goal of the 1994/1995 Premier League campaign against Newcastle United in a 3-1 defeat at Filbert Street in August 1994?

562. When Leicester beat Arsenal 2-1 at home in November 1994 which Arsenal player scored the first goal for Leicester?

563. From which club did Leicester sign Mark Draper in 1994?

564. To which club did Leicester sell Franz Carr in 1994?

545. How many Premier League matches did Leicester win during this season?

566. Who scored two goals in Leicester's 4-3 win over Southampton at home in October 1994?

567. Who made the most Premier League appearances for Leicester during this season?

568. In Leicester's memorable 4-4 draw at Aston Villa in February 1995, who scored a brace for Leicester?

569. Against which club did Ian Ormondroyd score his first goal of the season for the Foxes in September 1994 in a 3-0 away win.

570. Who was Leicester's top goal scorer this season?

1980s

571. Whom did Leicester beat 3-0 at Filbert Street on the first day of the 1980s?

572. Who was Leicester's top goalscorer for the 1980/1981 season in Division One?

573. Who was the future England international that Leicester signed from Alvechurch and who made his debut in 1982?

574. How many League goals did Gary Lineker score in the 1982/1983 season in Division Two - 26, 36 or 46?

575. From which club did Leicester sign Ian Banks for the 1983/1984 season?

576. At what ground did Leicester play their away FA Cup third round tie against Burton Albion on 5 January 1985 when they won 6-1?

577. Against which club did Gary Lineker score his last competitive goal for Leicester City on 6 May 1985?

578. Who was Leicester's top goalscorer in the 1985/1986 season?

579. In 1986 the lowest ever League Cup attendance at Filbert Street was 5,884, against which Welsh club?

580. Who was Leicester's top goalscorer in the 1988/1989 season?

LEAGUE CUP WINNERS 1997

581. Which company were sponsors of the League Cup when Leicester won it in 1997?

582. Whom did Leicester beat in the second round of the 1996/1997 League Cup?

583. Who scored Leicester's first goal of the Cup run that saw them go all the way to Wembley in 1997?

584. What was the score of Leicester's fourth round League Cup tie against Manchester United at Flibert Street on 27 November 1996?

585. Whom did Leicester beat on the away goal rule in the League Cup semi-final of 1997?

586. Who is missing from the starting line-up for the first drawn League Cup final match of 1997 between Middlesbrough and Leicester - Keller, Whitlow, Kaamark, Lennon, Walsh, Prior, Izzet, Parker, Claridge and Heskey?

587. At what ground was the League Cup final replay held in 1997?

588. Whom did Leicester knock out of the League Cup in the fifth round in 1997?

589. Neil Lennon scored one goal in the League Cup run of 1996/1997, against which team?

590. Which Leicester player scored the only penalty of the 1996/1997 League Cup run against at Filbert Street on 17 September 1996?

LEN GLOVER

591. From which club did Leicester sign Len?

592. Len was best known for playing in what position?

593. How many goals did Len score in his 319 appearances for Leicester City - 30, 40 or 50?

594. How much did Leicester pay to sign Len?

595. Against which London club did Len made his Leicester City debut on 18 November 1967?

596. Against which local rivals did Len score his first goal for Leicester in a 3-1 victory at Filbert Street on 13 January 1968?

597. In which season did Len score his highest number of League and Cup goals in a campaign for Leicester?

598. Len scored the second goal in Leicester's League Cup, second round, second leg match against which London club on 18 September 1974 in a 2-1 Leicester win?

599. Against which club did Len score his last goal for Leicester on 18 January 1975 at Filbert Street in Division One?

600. When Len left Leicester he went to play in the USA. Which famous American club did he join?

JOHN SJOBERG

601. In what city was John born?

602. John joined Leicester in 1958 at the age of 17, but in what year did he make his competitive first team debut?

603. John scored his first League goal for Leicester in 1964, against which club?

604. In John's best season as a goalscorer he scored six League and Cup goals, but which season was this?

605. What negative contribution did John make when Leicester lost 5-1 at West Bromwich Albion on 22 April 1966?

606. Against which east coast club did John score his first Leicester goal of the 1970s, in a 4-1 away defeat on 14 March 1970?

607. How many competitive goals did John Sjoberg score for Leicester City - 18, 19 or 20?

608. John scored his last goal for Leicester in a 1-1 away draw on 1 January 1972, against which Yorkshire club?

609. How many managers did John play for while he was at Leicester City FC?

610. What club did John sign for when he left Leicester in 1973?

DEREK DOUGAN

611. In what year was Derek born - 1935, 1937 or 1939?

612. From which team did Leicester sign Derek?

613. What nationality was Derek - English, Irish or Welsh?

614. Against which team did Derek make his Foxes debut in August 1965?

615. True or false: Derek scored 35 League goals for the Foxes during his career?

616. For which Midlands team did Derek play between 1961 and 1963?

617. What was Derek's well-known nickname?

618. How many full international caps did Derek win for his country - 33, 43 or 53?

619. Which Midlands club did Derek join when he left Leicester City?

620. In what position did Derek play during his playing days?

DIVISION TWO CHAMPIONS 1971

621.   How many points separated Leicester from the club
        that finished as runners-up in Division Two in 1971?

622.   Whom did Leicester beat 2-1 away to seal the Division
        Two Championship of 1971?

623.   Which player played in every League game of the
        1970/1971 season?

624.   Leicester lost 1-0 on the opening day of the
        1970/1971 season at Filbert Street to the team that
        went on to finish third in Division Two. Which team
        was that?

625.   Who was Leicester's top goalscorer when they won the
        Division Two Championship in 1971?

626.   How many times did Leicester win 1-0 in the
        1970/1971 Division Two Championship winning season
        - 10, 11 or 12?

627.   Who was the second top goalscorer for Leicester in the
        League in the 1970/1971 Division Two Championship
        winning season, having scored eight goals?

628.   Leicester went on an unbeaten run between 6
        February and the end of the season that helped them
        claim the the Division Two title. Which Midlands club
        was the last team to beat Leicester that season?

629.   Who was Leicester's captain when they won the
        1970/1971 Division Two Championship?

630.   Leicester conceded fewer goals than any other side in
        Division Two in 1970/1971. How many - 25, 30 or 35?

NATIONALITIES - 2

Match up the player with his nationality

631.	James Chambers	Hungarian
632.	Hossein Kaebi	English
633.	James Wesolowski	Danish
634.	Shaun Newton	Dutch
635.	Carl Cort	Bulgarian
636.	Martin Fulop	English
637.	Radostin Kishishev	English
638.	Sergio Hellings	Iranian
639.	Stephen Clemence	Australian
640.	Jimmy Nielsen	English

LEICESTER IN THE LEAGUE CUP

641. Who scored a hat-trick in Leicester's first ever game in the League Cup on 12 October 1960 in a 4-1 win against Mansfield Town at Filbert Street?

642. What was the aggregate score of the two-legged League Cup final when Leicester beat Stoke City in 1964?

643. In 1969/1970, Leicester finally overcame Bristol City after two 0-0 draws in the second round of the League Cup. What was the final score when the Foxes did win the tie?

644. Who was Leicester's top scorer in the 1970/1971 League Cup campaign?

645. What was the furthest round that Leicester managed to reach in the 1970s?

646. Who scored Leicester's first League Cup goal of the 1980s in a 4-0 win against Preston North End at Filbert Street on 28 October 1981?

647. In what year of the 1980s did Leicester have their best League Cup run of the decade, when they reached the fourth round?

648. Who knocked Leicester out of the League Cup the year before Leicester won the trophy in 1997?

649. Who knocked Leicester out of the League Cup when they were holders in the 1997/1998 season?

650. Which team did Leicester defeat in the League Cup runs of both 1998/1999 and 1999/2000, resulting in the Foxes playing at Wembley?

BIG WINS

*Match up the fixture with the final winning
scoreline for Leicester*

651.	v. Sheffield Wednesday (Away) December 2006, Championship	5-1
652.	v. West Bromwich Albion (Home) September 1959, Division One	6-1
653.	v. Lincoln City (Home) December 1955, Division Two	5-2
654.	v. Sunderland (Home) March 2000, Premiership	5-0
655.	v. Ipswich Town (Home) January 1974, Division One	4-0
656.	v. Rochdale (Away) September 1993, Division One	4-1
657.	v. Sheffield Wednesday (Home) January 1987, Division One	5-0
658.	v. Coventry City (Home) December 1984, Division One	6-1
659.	v. Aston Villa (Home) October 1984, Division One	6-1
660.	v. Fulham (Home) August 1952, Division Two	5-0

DIVISION ONE PLAY-OFF WINNERS 1996

661. In what League position did Leicester finish in 1996 to qualify for the play-offs?

662. Leicester went on a winning run of how many games at the end of the 1995/1996 season to secure their play-off place?

663. What was the final score of the play-off semi-final first leg against Stoke City at Filbert Street?

664. Which of Leicester's two play-off opponents had they lost to twice when they met in the League in the 1995/1996 season?

665. Leicester's top scorer of the 1995/1996 season failed to score for them in the play-offs. Who was that?

666. Who was Leicester's top scorer in the 1996 Division One play-offs?

667. Who was the goalkeeper that Leicester brought on just before they scored the winner in the Division One play-off final of 1996?

668. What nationality was the goalkeeper that Leicester brought on late in the play-off final of 1996?

669. What was the aggregate score of the three League and play-off meetings between Leicester and Crystal Palace during 1995/1996?

670. What was the attendance of the 1995 play-off final - 68,147, 73,573 or 73,802?

STEVE CLARIDGE

671. In what year was Steve born in Portsmouth - 1964, 1965 or 1966?

672. Against which team did Steve score the winning goal in the 2-1 play-off final victory in May 1996?

673. Leicester beat Blackburn 4-2 away in May 1997. Steve scored one of the goals, but which player scored a brace for the Foxes?

674. In what year did Steve join Leicester?

675. True or false: during 1996/1997 Steve got sent off twice?

676. How many League goals did Steve score for Leicester during his career?

677. On 5 March 1997, Steve scored the only goal in a 1-0 home win against which team?

678. On Boxing Day 1996, Steve scored away at Liverpool, but which future Foxes striker scored for the Reds that evening?

679. How many League goals did Steve score for Leicester during 1996/1997 - 10, 11 or 12?

680. When Steve left Leicester in 1998, which Midlands team did he join?

KEITH WELLER

681. In what year did Keith join Leicester City?

682. From which club did Leicester sign Keith?

683. Against which club did Keith score his first goal for Leicester City?

684. At which club did Keith begin his football career?

685. What accessory was Keith wearing when he scored his last goal for Leicester in 1979?

686. Against which club did Keith once refuse to play the second half of a League match in 1974?

687. Keith won the Goal of the Season award in 1974, but against which club did he score that FA Cup goal?

688. In what year did Keith win a European Cup Winners' Cup medal?

689. In 2002, Keith was diagnosed with a rare form of cancer. To the nearest thousand, how much money did Leicester City fans raise to fund his treatment?

690. How old was Keith when he passed away in November 2004?

PAUL RAMSEY

691. Where in Northern Ireland was Paul born?

692. In which season did Paul make his Leicester City debut?

693. How many Northern Ireland caps did Paul win as a Leicester player?

694. Against which club did Paul score his first goal for Leicester City in 1983?

695. Which Leicester manager gave Paul his Leicester debut?

696. In which season did Paul score his highest total of goals in a campaign for Leicester when he hit the back of the net six times?

697. Paul scored twice in a game only once during his Leicester career, against which club?

698. Against which club did Paul score his last goal for Leicester on 2 May 1990?

699. How many appearances did Paul make for Leicester City - 298, 308 or 318?

700. To which club did Paul transfer in 1991?

LEICESTER V. WOLVES

701. Who scored Leicester's equaliser in the 1-1 draw between the Foxes and Wolves at Molineaux on 4 May 2003?

702. Leicester first played Wolverhampton Wanderers in the League on 6 October 1906, but what was the final score of that home match for the Foxes?

703. What was the final score when Leicester City visited Wolverhampton Wanderers on 9 December 2006 in the Coca-Cola Championship?

704. In what year did Leicester City first beat Wolverhampton Wanderers away from home?

705. What was the final score of the first ever Premier League meeting between Wolverhampton Wanderers and Leicester City?

706. Who scored the winning goal when Leicester won the first meeting against Wolverhampton Wanderers to be played at the Walkers Stadium on 28 September 2002?

707. In what year did Leicester and Wolves first meet in the top flight of English football?

708. Which Leicester player scored a hat-trick when the Foxes beat Wolves 3-2 at Filbert Street in Division One on 22 March 1975?

709. Leicester paid a then record fee of £5,000,000 to Wolverhampton Wanderers in July 2000 to sign which player?

710. Which Irishman scored 41 goals for Leicester before joining Wolves in 1967?

DAVID GIBSON

711. From which Scottish club did Leicester sign David?

712. In what year did David make his Leicester debut?

713. According to a questionnaire answered by David, which player was the toughest opponent that he played against?

714. What fee did Leicester pay to sign David?

715. Against which Midlands club did David score his first goal for Leicester City?

716. Who was David's favourite strike partner at Leicester City?

717. In which season did David score his highest League and Cup tally for a campaign in a Leicester shirt?

718. Against which Yorkshire club did David score his last competitive goal for Leicester City?

719. What club did David join when he left Leicester City in 1970?

720. At what club did David end his playing career in 1973?

PREMIER LEAGUE 2000/2001

721. In what position in the League did Leicester City finish?

722. Against which team did Leicester record their first win of the season, a 1-0 away win?

723. Following on from the previous question, which player scored the goal?

724. In September 2000, Ade Akinbiyi and Matt Elliott scored in a 2-1 home win, against which team?

725. In December 2000, Leicester beat West Ham United 2-1 at home, but which players scored the goals?

726. Which forward finished as top League goalscorer with nine goals?

727. Which defender was the only Leicester player to appear in all 38 League matches, scoring two goals?

728. How many Premier League games did Leicester win during the season - 10, 12 or 14?

729. Which player did Leicester buy in December 2000 for £3 million?

730. In the Foxes' last game of the season, which London team did they beat 4-2?

JOHN PATRICK O'NEILL

731. What subject did John study at Loughborough University?

732. Against which Lancashire club did John make his Leicester City debut?

733. What international record does John hold in relation to the Foxes?

734. Against which country did John win his first Northern Ireland cap as a Leicester player in March 1980?

735. Against which Yorkshire club did John score his first goal for Leicester?

736. John scored his first two League goals for Leicester in the same season, but what season was that?

737. Against which club did John score his one and only FA Cup goal in 1982?

738. Against which club did John score his last goal for Leicester on 18 April 1987?

739. In which season did John play in every single game for Leicester?

740. What club did John move to when he left Leicester in 1987?

LEICESTER V. BIRMINGHAM CITY

741. In 1986, Leicester's biggest win of the season was at home to Birmingham, but what was the final score?

742. In what year did Leicester Fosse and Small Heath (as Birmingham City was then called) first meet in the Football League - 1897, 1904 or 1907?

743. In what year did Leicester and the newly named Birmingham City first meet in the FA Cup - 1905, 1910 or 1915?

744. In what year did Leicester City FC first meet the newly named Birmingham City FC in the Football League?

745. Which player did Leicester sign from Birmingham in 1996, who went on to score for Leicester against his former club in a 3-0 victory at Filbert Street on 27 April that year?

746. Leicester's biggest win of the 1985/1986 season was against Birmingham City at Filbert Street on 12 March 1986, but what was the final score of that game?

747. On 2 January 1999, Leicester knocked Birmingham out of the FA Cup in the third round, but what was the final score of that Filbert Street tie?

748. Leicester met Birmingham at The Walkers Stadium on 13 December 2003 in the Premier League, but what was the final score of that game?

749. What happened to Birmingham at the end of the season in which Leicester beat them 2-0 with a double strike by Ali Mauchlen at Filbert Street on 25 March 1989?

750. On 6 April 1974, Leicester and Birmingham played out a 3-3 draw at Filbert Street. Who scored two goals for the Foxes that day?

NEIL LENNON

751. In what year was Neil born - 1969, 1970 or 1971?

752. Against which team did Neil score in the 3-3 away draw in April 1998?

753. Which manager signed Neil for the Foxes in 1996?

754. In April 2000, Neil scored in a 2-2 away draw at Villa Park, but which other player scored for the Foxes?

755. During March 1999, against which team did Neil score in a 1-1 Premier League draw?

756. How many League goals did Neil score for the Foxes during his career - 6, 16 or 26?

757. In what position did Neil play for the Foxes?

758. What nationality is Neil - Welsh, English or Northern Irish?

759. For which team did Neil play between 1990 and 1996?

760. Which team did Neil sign for during June 2007?

LEAGUE APPEARANCES - 1

Match up the player with the number of
League appearances made for the club

761.	Mark Bright	596 (3)
762.	David Kelly	195 (5)
763.	Paul Ramsey	26 (16)
764.	John Bamber	286
765.	Gary Mills	63 (3)
766.	John Ridley	58 (3)
767.	Graham Cross	37
768.	Peter Shilton	113
769.	David Speedie	278 (12)
770.	Mark Venus	17 (7)

SQUAD NUMBERS 2009/2010

Match up the player with his squad number for the season

771.	Chris Powell	1
772.	Bruno Berner	25
773.	Andy King	8
774.	Robbie Neilson	29
775.	Aleksandar Tunchev	6
776.	Luke O'Neill	10
777.	Jack Hobbs	2
778.	Wayne Brown	5
779.	Chris Weale	15
780.	Matt Oakley	20

LEAGUE CUP WINNERS 2000

781. Which manager guided the club to this success?

782. Which London club did City beat 7-5 on aggregate in the second round?

783. True or false: Leicester beat Leeds United 4-2 on penalties during December 1999?

784. Which London club did Leicester beat 3-0 on penalties after a 3-3 draw during January 2000 in the quarter-final?

785. Following on from the previous question, which City striker scored twice in the match?

786. Which player scored in the 1-0 semi-final, second leg win during February 2000?

787. True or false: the final was played at The Millennium Stadium?

788. Can you name seven of the starting eleven that played in the League Cup final?

789. Which team did Leicester beat 2-1 in the final?

790. Following on from the previous question, which player scored both goals?

CITY HONOURS - 1

Match up the honour achieved with the correct year

791. **League Cup Winners**   *1994*

792. **First Division Play-Off Winners**   *2003*

793. **First Division Runners-Up**   *1997*

794. **First Division Runners-Up**   *1964*

795. **FA Cup Runners-Up**   *1929*

796. **League Cup Winners**   *1996*

797. **Charity Shield Winners**   *1969*

798. **First Division Play-Off Winners**   *1963*

799. **FA Cup Runners-Up**   *2000*

800. **League Cup Winners**   *1971*

PREMIER LEAGUE 1996/1997

801. Who scored Leicester's first two goals of the 1996/1997 season in a 2-1 win against Southampton at Filbert Street on 21 August 1996?

802. Which were the two teams that succumbed to 4-2 defeats by Leicester during the 1996/1997 season?

803. Who scored the only Leicester hat-trick in the Premier League during 1996/1997?

804. What was the final score when Leicester played their League Cup final opponents Middlesbrough in the Premier League away game on 3 December 1996?

805. Leicester beat high-flying Newcastle United in the Premier League on 26 October 1996 at Filbert Street, but what was the final score of that match?

806. Who scored Leicester's goal in their 3-1 defeat to Manchester United at Old Trafford on 30 November 1996?

807. Who scored his last goal for Leicester in the Foxes' 3-1 win at Wimbledon on 1 March 1997, his only Premier League goal of the 1996/1997 season?

808. Who scored his last Premier League goal for Leicester City in the last game of the 1996/1997 season against Blackburn Rovers?

809. Who made the most Premier League appearances for Leicester during the 1996/1997 season?

810. In what position did Leicester finish in the Premier League in 1996/1997?

POSITIONS IN THE LEAGUE - 2

*Match up the season with the position
in which Leicester finished*

811.	1986/1987	Division One	11th
812.	1984/1985	Division One	1st
813.	1982/1983	Division Two	21st
814.	1980/1981	Division One	18th
815.	1978/1979	Division Two	20th
816.	1976/1977	Division One	17th
817.	1974/1975	Division One	15th
818.	1972/1973	Division One	21st
819.	1970/1971	Division Two	3rd
820.	1968/1969	Division One	16th

FRANK SINCLAIR

821.   While he was at Chelsea, Frank played six games on loan at another Midlands club. Which one?

822.   In what year did Frank sign for Leicester City?

823.   Against which club did Frank score his first Premier League goal for Leicester?

824.   Where in London was Frank born?

825.   For which country did Frank play international football?

826.   How many yellow cards did Frank receive during the 2001/2002 Premier League season for Leicester City - 4, 6 or 8?

827.   Frank scored just one goal for Leicester during the 2002/2003 Football League Championship season, in a 3-2 away win against which club?

828.   How many red cards did Frank receive while playing for Leicester City?

829.   Which club did Frank join when he left Leicester in 2004?

830.   Which club did Frank join in 2007?

ARTHUR ROWLEY

831.   Where was Arthur born?

832.   From which club did Leicester sign Arthur?

833.   In what year did Arthur make his goalscoring Leicester City debut?

834.   What honours did Arthur win with Leicester City?

835.   In which season did Arthur score 44 League goals for Leicester City?

836.   In 1952, Arthur scored four of Leicester's six goals against which London club on 25 August at Filbert Street?

837.   How many goals did Arthur score for Leicester City during his career?

838.   Against which Midlands club did Arthur score his last goal for Leicester?

839.   Arthur was Leicester's top scorer in every season he was at the club, except for one - 1955/1956. Which player scored more goals for the Foxes than Arthur in that season?

840.   Which club did Arthur join when he left Leicester in 1958?

LAWRENCE MAY

841. In which season did Lawrence make his Leicester City debut?

842. Against which club did Lawrence score his first goal for the Foxes?

843. In which season did Lawrence play in every League and Cup match for Leicester?

844. How many times did Lawrence experience promotion to Division One whilst playing for Leicester?

845. Which manager gave Lawrence his Leicester City debut?

846. Lawrence's best League goal tally for Leicester was four goals, which he achieved twice, once in 1978/1979 and again when?

847. Where was Lawrence born?

848. What club did Lawrence turn down in favour of joining Leicester?

849. Against which club did Lawrence score his last goal for Leicester?

850. Which club did Lawrence move to when he left Leicester in 1983?

PREMIER LEAGUE 2001/2002

851.   In which month of 2001 was Peter Taylor sacked as
        Leicester manager?

852.   Leicester's relegation was sealed after a 1-0 defeat to
        which club on 6 April 2002?

853.   Name the two people who took the position of
        assistant manager for Leicester after Peter Taylor left
        the club?

854.   When Leicester beat Tottenham Hotspur on the last
        day of the season, how many Premier League games
        had they previously won during 2001/2002?

855.   On what date did Leicester play their final game at
        Filbert Street?

856.   Leicester left Filbert Street in 2002. For how many
        years was Filbert Street Leicester's home?

857.   What was the score when Leicester travelled to Derby
        County on 15 September 2001?

858.   Which club was relegated with Leicester and Derby at
        the end of the 2001/2002 season?

859.   Leicester City versus Middlesbrough attracted the
        lowest attendance of the season in the Premier
        League. What was the final score of that match?

860.   Who scored Leicester's penultimate goal at Filbert
        Street?

LEAGUE GOALSCORERS - 2

*Match up the player with the total number of
League goals scored for Leicester City*

861.	Matt Elliott	6
862.	Ricky Hill	21
863.	Ernest Hine	25
864.	Tony Cottee	95
865.	Gary Lineker	27
866.	James Walsh	5
867.	Julian Joachim	148
868.	Dennis Rofe	0
869.	Mike Newell	27
870.	William Hughes	79

LEAGUE APPEARANCES - 2

*Match up the player with the number of
League appearances made for the club*

871.	Gary Lineker	93 (8)
872.	David Nish	190 (10)
873.	Alistair Brown	2
874.	Stephen Whitworth	193
875.	Richard Norman	352 (1)
876.	John Farmer	127
877.	James Quinn	228
878.	Alan Smith	303
879.	Howard Riley	13 (18)
880.	William Cunningham	187 (7)

GARY McALLISTER

881. Leicester signed Gary from his hometown club, but which club was that?

882. In what year did Gary sign for Leicester?

883. Against which club did Gary score his first goal for Leicester?

884. In which season was Gary Leicester's top scorer in Division Two?

885. How many Scotland caps did Gary win as a Leicester player?

886. Who was Leicester's top goalscorer during Gary's first season with the club?

887. How many goals did Gary score for Leicester City - 47, 57 or 67?

888. In what year did Gary leave Leicester City?

889. Against which club did Gary score his last goal for Leicester?

890. Which club did Gary join when he left Leicester City?

LEICESTER V. DERBY COUNTY

891. What was the final score at the first ever Premier League meeting between Leicester City and Derby County?

892. What was the final score at the first ever Football League meeting between Leicester Fosse and Derby County at Filbert Street?

893. When Derby won the Division One title in both 1971/1972 and 1974/1975, what was the best result that Leicester achieved against them in both of those seasons?

894. Leicester and Derby only met once at Filbert Street in the League throughout the whole of the 1950s and 1960s. What was the final score of that meeting in 1953?

895. When Leicester and Derby met in the second round of the League Cup in 1978, Leicester were knocked out by what scoreline?

896. On 15 September 2001, Leicester travelled to Pride Park and claimed a memorable 3-2 victory against Derby County. Which former Ram scored two goals for Leicester that day?

897. On 14 September 2002, Leicester and Derby met in Division One at the Walkers Stadium. What was the final score of that win for the Foxes?

898. On 11 August 2004, Leicester travelled to Pride Park and won 2-1. Who came off the Leicester bench to score the winning goal?

899. Which former Derby defender played for Leicester against the Rams on 28 October 2000 at Filbert Street?

900. Who scored for Leicester in the 1-1 draw with Championship-chasing Derby at the Walkers Stadium on Friday 6 April 2007?

JULIAN JOACHIM

901. Julian was born in Peterborough, in what year - 1972, 1974 or 1976?

902. Julian made his debut as an 18-year-old in a 2-1 home win against which club?

903. How many League goals did Julian score during his Foxes career - 25, 35 or 45?

904. Which Foxes manager handed Julian his Leicester debut?

905. Against which London team did Julian score a brace in September 1994 in a 3-1 win?

906. In August 1993, Leicester beat Millwall in a 4-0 home win. Julian scored one goal, but can you name the other   two players that scored?

907. Julian left Leicester in February 1996 and joined which Midlands team?

908. Julian scored a brace in the 3-2 away win against which team in April 1994, with Paul Kerr scoring the other goal?

909. In March 1994, Leicester beat Birmingham City 3-0 away from home. Julian scored one goal, but which other two Foxes players scored?

910. Which team did Julian sign for from Boston United in August 2006?

MIKE STRINGFELLOW

911. Where was Mike born?

912. By what nickname was Mike known to Leicester fans?

913. What phrase did Jimmy Bloomfield often use to describe Mike and his importance to the team?

914. How much did Leicester pay Mike's former club to sign him?

915. What club did Mike leave to join Leicester City?

916. Against which club did Mike make his Leicester City debut?

917. Against which club did Mike score his first Leicester goal on the first day of the 1962/1963 season?

918. For how many seasons did Mike play for Leicester?

919. How many goals did Mike score for Leicester City - 87, 97 or 107?

920. In which season was Mike Leicester's top goalscorer?

HAT-TRICK HEROES

921. Who scored a hat-trick for Leicester against Sunderland in a 5-2 victory at Filbert Street on 5 March 2000?

922. Who scored four hat-tricks for Leicester during the 1952/1953 season?

923. Who scored a hat-trick in Leicester's 4-0 thrashing of Derby County on 23 October 1982?

924. Who scored a hat-trick when Leicester thrashed Wolverhampton Wanderers 5-1 on 10 December 1983?

925. Who scored a second-half hat-trick for Leicester when they beat Stoke City 4-2 in the Coca-Cola Championship on Tuesday 9 August 2005?

926. Who scored a hat-trick for Leicester when they beat Portsmouth 4-2 at Filbert Street on 30 August 1995?

927. Who scored a hat-trick for Leicester when they beat Newcastle United 5-4 in Division Two on 1 December 1990 at Filbert Street? (A bonus if you can also name the player who scored a hat-trick for the losing side that day.)

928. On 3 January 1987, Leicester stuffed Sheffield Wednesday 6-1 at Filbert Street, but who scored a hat-trick for the Foxes in that match?

929. On 14 January 1984, Leicester travelled to Notts County and won 5-2 with the help of a hat-trick from which Foxes striker?

930. Who scored a hat-trick for Leicester on the last day of the 1980/1981 season in a 3-2 win at Norwich City?

NIGEL PEARSON

931. What is Nigel's middle name – Graham, Gary or George?

932. In which year was Nigel appointed as Leicester City boss?

933. True or false: Leicester City won the League One title in Nigel's first season in charge at the club?

934. Against which team did Leicester play during Nigel's first game in charge of The Foxes, winning 2-0 at The Walkers Stadium?

935. In which position did Nigel play during his playing days – defender, midfielder or striker?

936. True or false: Nigel won the League One manager of the month award in his first season at Leicester City?

937. At which club did Nigel start his managerial career, managing them during the 1998/1999 season?

938. From which manager did Nigel take over as Leicester City manager?

939. In which year was Nigel born in Nottingham – 1961, 1962 or 1963?

940. True or false: Nigel played for The Foxes during his playing career?

POT LUCK - 3

941. How many League goals did Robert Davison score for Leicester during his career?

942. Which manager signed Peter Eccles, who only made one appearance for the club?

943. In what position did Reg Osborne play for the Foxes?

944. From which team did David Pleat sign Marc North during March 1989?

945. Against which club did Mark Draper make his debut during August 1994?

946. In what position did Chris Garland play for the Foxes?

947. Which player scored twice on his debut in May 1969 at home to Sunderland?

948. Which player was Leicester's first £2 million signing, costing £2.05 million?

949. Against which club did Kevin Russell make his debut in August 1989?

950. In what position did Steve Whitworth play for the Foxes?

LEAGUE ONE CHAMPIONS - 2008/2009

951. How many of The Foxes 46 League games did Leicester City win – 23, 25 or 27?

952. Which team finished as runners-up in League One, 7 points behind The Foxes?

953. With which team did Leicester share a 1-1 draw away from home during Boxing Day 2008?

954. True or false: Leicester City were unbeaten in all 5 League matches during December 2008?

955. Which London club did Leicester beat 3-1 away during September 2008 with Lloyd Dyer, Matty Fryatt and Andy King scoring the goals for the Foxes?

956. Can you name the midfielder that scored a brace for Leicester City in the 4-0 away win over Cheltenham Town during August 2008?

957. Which defender did Leicester City sign in August 2008 from Charlton Athletic?

958. How many League goals did Matty Fryatt score for The Foxes in his 46 League appearances, finishing the clubs highest scorer this season – 23, 25 or 27?

959. Which manager guided the club to this success?

960. Which team did Leicester beat 3-0 away from home on the last day of the season?

BOBBY ROBERTS

961. From what Scottish club did Leicester sign Bobby?

962. In what year did Bobby make his Leicester City debut?

963. Bobby became Leicester City's most expensive signing at the time. How much did he cost manager Matt Gillies?

964. When he joined Leicester, Bobby took over the number four shirt from which player?

965. Bobby scored his first and second goals for Leicester in the same match. Who was Leicester visiting in their 3-0 win on 26 December 1963?

966. In which season did Bobby finish with his best goal tally for Leicester?

967. Against which club did Bobby score his last goal for Leicester in a 1-0 away win on 27 March 1970?

968. How many goals did Bobby score in the 281 matches he played for Leicester - 36, 46 or 56?

969. In which season of his Leicester career did Bobby play in every League and Cup match for the club?

970. What club did Bobby join when he left Leicester in 1970?

CITY HONOURS - 2

Match up the honour achieved with the correct year

971.	Second Division Champions	1949
972.	First Division Play-Off Runners-Up	1957
973.	Second Division Champions	1961
974.	FA Cup Runners-Up	1937
975.	Second Division Champions	1925
976.	League Cup Runners-Up	1971
977.	Second Division Champions	1954
978.	FA Cup Runners-Up	1980
979.	Second Division Champions	2003
980.	Second Division Champions	1999

GRAHAM CROSS

981. How many appearances did Graham make for Leicester City?

982. Against which of Leicester's local rivals did Graham make his goalscoring Leicester debut?

983. In which season did Graham notch up his best goal tally for the Foxes?

984. How many goals did Graham score for Leicester in the 1970s?

985. How many goals did Graham score in his entire Leicester career?

986. In which two consecutive seasons did Graham play in every League game for the club, only missing one League Cup match and totalling 106 appearances?

987. In what season did Graham make his last appearance for Leicester?

988. Which club did Graham help to win the Division Three title after he had left Leicester City?

989. Which club did Graham help to promotion in 1978?

990. Which club did Graham fail to save from relegation when he joined them in 1979?

WHERE DID THEY GO? - 2

*Match up the player with the club he
moved to from Leicester*

991.	Spencer Prior	Burnley
992.	Momo Sylla	Plymouth Argyle
993.	David Rennie	Dundee United
994.	Tony Spearing	Wolves
995.	Andy Johnson	Port Vale
996.	Nicky Cross	Barnsley
997.	Frank Sinclair	Kilmarnock
998.	Patrick McCarthy	Derby County
999.	Arnar Gunnlaugsson	Leeds United
1000.	Mark Venus	Charlton Athletic

ANSWERS

THE CLUB - RECORDS & HISTORY

1. The Foxes, Fosse, The Filberts
2. 1884
3. 1891
4. Ade Akinbiyi
5. Portsmouth
6. Arthur Rowley
7. Liverpool
8. Tottenham Hotpsur
9. 1961/1962: European Cup Winners Cup
10. 2002

MUZZY IZZET

11. 1974
12. Chelsea
13. Sheffield United
14. Ade Akinbiyi
15. Midfield
16. Tottenham Hotspur
17. Martin O'Neill
18. Turkey
19. Birmingham City
20. Knee injury

MANAGERS

21. David Pleat   1987 to 1991
22. Brian Little   1991 to 1994
23. Martin O'Neill   1995 to 2000
24. Johnny Duncan   1946 to 1949
25. Frank McLintock 1977 to 1978

26.	Peter Hodge	1932 to 1934
27.	Craig Levein	2004 to 2006
28.	Matt Gillies	1959 to 1968
29.	Gordon Milne	1982 to 1986
30.	Jimmy Bloomfield	1971 to 1977

MARTIN O'NEILL

31. 1995
32. OBE
33. 1997 and 2000
34. 1995/1996
35. UEFA Cup
36. Aston Villa
37. 64
38. Nottingham Forest
39. Aston Martin or Midas
40. Celtic

WHERE DID THEY GO? - 1

41.	Gareth Williams	Watford
42.	Ian Walker	Bolton Wanderers
43.	Dion Dublin	Celtic
44.	Brian Deane	West Ham United
45.	Andy Impey	Nottingham Forest
46.	Spencer Prior	Derby County
47.	Mark Draper	Aston Villa
48.	Mark Venus	Wolverhampton Wanderers
49.	Russell Osman	Southampton
50.	Momo Sylla	Kilmarnock

GORDON BANKS

51. 1937
52. Goalkeeper
53. Chesterfield
54. 1959
55. 73
56. Matt Gillies
57. Football Writers' Player of the Year
58. True
59. 1963
60. Banks of England

THE CHAMPIONSHIP 2006/2007

61. Gareth McAuley
62. Ipswich Town
63. Rob Kelly
64. Iain Hume
65. Patrick Kisnorbo
66. 10
67. Leeds United
68. Levi Porter
69. Gareth Williams
70. Mark Yeates

GARY LINEKER

71. 1960
72. Oldham Athletic
73. Winston
74. Links, Winston, The Queen Mother of Football
75. 95

76. *Jock Wallace*

77. *Notts County*

78. *Everton*

79. *Barcelona*

80. *48*

LEAGUE CUP WINNERS 1964

81. *Aldershot*

82. *Matt Gillies*

83. *True*

84. *FA Cup*

85. *West Ham United*

86. *6-3 (4-3 and 2-0)*

87. *True*

88. *Gordon Banks, John Sjoberg, Colin Appleton, Derek Dougan, Ian King, Graham Cross, Howard Riley, Terry Heath, Ken Keyworth, Dave Gibson and Mike Stringfellow*

89. *Dave Gibson*

90. *Stoke City*

EMILE HESKEY

91. *1978*

92. *Queens Park Rangers*

93. *10*

94. *Norwich City*

95. *Bruno*

96. *Chelsea*

97. *Liverpool*

98. *Tony Cottee*

99.   Mark McGhee

100.   Wigan Athletic

LEICESTER CITY V. NOTTINGHAM FOREST

101.   1915 (20 February; Nottingham Forest 1, Leicester Fosse 3)

102.   Steve Lynex

103.   It was their first ever Sunday game

104.   Gary Lineker

105.   1996/1997 (Leicester finished 9th, Forest finished 20th)

106.   Paul Groves

107.   2-1

108.   Leicester City 4, Nottingham Forest 2

109.   Mike Stringfellow

110.   Gary Charles

ALAN YOUNG

111.   Watford

112.   15 (14 League 1 Cup)

113.   Oldham Athletic

114.   Wolverhampton Wanderers (2-0 win, Filbert Street)

115.   Shrewsbury Town

116.   Kevin MacDonald

117.   Charlton Athletic

118.   Kirkcaldy

119.   29

120.   Sheffield United

CITY TRANSFERS

121. £1 million
122. Lincoln City
123. Blackpool
124. Everton
125. £500,000
126. Gary McAllister
127. Luton Town
128. Lens
129. Crewe Alexandra
130. £50,000

1970s

131. Sunderland
132. Sheffield United
133. 4 (Frank O'Farrell, Jimmy Bloomfield, Frank McLintock and Jock Wallace)
134. The FA Charity Shield
135. Burnley
136. November 1974
137. Newcastle United (3-0)
138. Frank Worthington (14 goals)
139. West Ham United
140. 7 (1971/72, 72/73, 73/74, 74/75, 75/76, 76/77 and 77/78)

NATIONALITIES - 1

141. Rab Douglas   Scottish
142. Andy King   Welsh
143. Jimmy Nielsen   Danish

144.	Tony Cottee	English
145.	Bruno N'Gotty	French
146.	Elvis Hammond	Ghanaian
147.	Paul Henderson	Australian
148.	Ricky Sappleton	Jamaican
149.	Iain Hume	Canadian
150.	Emile Heskey	English

MANAGERS OF THE FOXES

151. Frank Gardner
152. Tottenham Hotspur
153. Matt Gillies
154. Jon Sammels
155. 1991
156. Gordon Lee
157. Frank O'Farrell
158. Mark McGhee
159. David Hall
160. Martin Allen

POT LUCK - 1

161. Mark Draper
162. Striker
163. Arsenal
164. Gordon Banks
165. 14
166. Trevor Hebberd
167. Graham Cross
168. Left back
169. 66

170.   Iwan Roberts

BOBBY SMITH

171.   Hibernian

172.   1979 (1 January, v. Oldham Athletic)

173.   1991 (28 December, v. Southend United)

174.   Carlisle United (1-0 win)

175.   1979/1980 (12 goals)

176.   1985/1986

177.   1986/1987 and 1987/1988

178.   Crystal Palace

179.   1995/1996

180.   Hibernian

LEICESTER V. ASTON VILLA

181.   Phil Gee

182.   1908 (Division 1, 31 October, 1-1 away draw)

183.   Stan Collymore

184.   Julian Joachim

185.   Ade Akinbiyi

186.   Steve Claridge

187.   Villa were relegated to Division 3

188.   Steve Lynex

189.   Ian Marshall

190.   Tony Cottee

PREMIER LEAGUE 1997/1998

191.   Martin O'Neill

192.   Blackburn Rovers

193.   Newcastle United

194.   Steve Walsh, Steve Guppy and Emile Heskey

195.   4-0 to Leicester

196.   Tony Cottee

197.   Emile Heskey, Matt Elliott and Steve Walsh

198.   Dennis Bergkamp

199   10th

200.   Theo Zagorakis

DAVID NISH

201.   3 December 1966, v. Stoke City

202.   1967/1968

203.   He was the youngest player to captain a team in an FA
        Cup final at the age of 21

204.   Burton-on-Trent

205.   League Division Two Championship in 1970/1971
        season

206.   West Ham United

207.   277

208.   Derby County

209.   £250,000

210.   Middlesbrough

ALAN BIRCHENALL

211.   East Ham

212.   Crystal Palace

213.   1945 (22 August)

214.   1971

215.   Chelsea (home, 1-1 draw, 30 October 1971)

216.   Leeds United

217.   Arsenal

218. *1977*

219. *176*

220. *Notts County*

FRANK WORTHINGTON

221. *1948*

222. *1972*

223. *Manchester United*

224. *210: 209 (1)*

225. *Striker*

226. *72*

227. *Jimmy Bloomfield*

228. *Stewart*

229. *Huddersfield Town*

230. *Tranmere Rovers*

IN WHAT YEAR?

231. *Frank McLintock was appointed manager*   *1977*

232. *Leonard Glover made his City debut against Arsenal at home*   *1967*

233. *Kevin Poole was born*   *1963*

234. *Ian Andrews made his City debut against Wolves*   *1984*

235. *James Walsh was born*   *1930*

236. *Norman Bullock took over as manager*   *1949*

237. *Dennis Rofe left for Chelsea*   *1980*

238. *Richard Smith was born*   *1970*

239. *George Meek joined from Leeds United*   *1960*

240. *Mike Newell scored on his City debut against Oldham Athletic*   *1987*

WHERE DID THEY COME FROM?

241.	Phil Gee	Derby County
242.	Stephen Clemence	Birmingham City
243.	Pat Byrne	Shelbourne
244.	Arthur Maw	Notts County
245.	Franz Carr	Sheffield United
246.	Carl Cort	Wolves
247.	Bob Hazell	Queens Park Rangers
248.	DJ Campbell	Birmingham City
249.	Allan Evans	Aston Villa
250.	Jon Sammels	Arsenal

LEICESTER IN THE FA CUP

251. Leatherhead
252. Mal Griffiths
253. Portsmouth (3-1)
254. Sheffield United
255. Ken Keyworth
256. Liverpool
257. Arsenal
258. Graham Cross (59)
259. Arthur Rowley
260. Norman Plumber

1990s

261. Portsmouth (3-2, Fratton Park)
262. Oxford United
263. Leicester City 5, Cambridge United 0
264. Portsmouth (1-0 and 2-2)
265. David Speedie

266. *Iwan Roberts (11 Goals: 9 League, 2 Cup)*
267. *Tottenham Hotspur*
268. *Steve Claridge (11 League goals)*
269. *Robbie Savage*
270. *Theo Zagorakis*

UNUSUAL RESULTS

271. *v. Manchester United (Home)*   **2-6**
January 1999, Premiership
272. *v. Fulham (Home)*   **3-3**
September 1979, Division Two
273. *v. Leeds United (Home)*   **4-3**
November 1989, Division Two
274. *v. West Ham United (Home)*   **5-4**
August 1966, Division One
275. *v. Watford (Home)*   **4-4**
December 1993, Division One
276. *v. Notts County (Home)*   **6-3**
September 1956, Division Two
277. *v. Fulham (Away)*   **6-4**
September 1952, Division Two
278. *v. Leyton Orient (Home)*   **5-3**
February 1979, Division Two
279. *v. Southampton (Away)*   **3-5**
April 1950, Division Two
280. *v. Newcastle United (Away)*   **4-5**
January 1990, Division Two

DIVISION TWO CHAMPIONS 1980
281. *Dennis Rofe*

282. Queens Park Rangers (4-1, Loftus Road, 25 August 1979)
283. Larry May
284. 3
285. Chelsea
286. Cardiff City, 12,877 (0-0 draw, 21 December 1979)
287. Sunderland and Birmingham City
288. Preston North End (2-1 defeat, Filbert Street, 29 March 1980)
289. Sunderland
290. Larry May, Mark Wallington and Alan Young

ALLY MAUCHLEN
291. 1960 (29 June)
292. Ayrshire (Kilwinning)
293. Motherwell
294. 1985
295. Chelsea
296. 1988/1989 (3 goals in Division 2, 1 in League Cup)
297. Brighton and Hove Albion (2-1 win, Filbert Street)
298. Brian Little
299. 238
300. 11

FRANK McLINTOCK
301. 1939
302. Scottish
303. Blackpool
304. False: 168
305. 1971

306. 25

307. 1964

308. MBE

309. Matt Gillies

310. Queens Park Rangers

JON SAMMELS

311. Ipswich

312. Arsenal

313. £100,000

314. Liverpool (FA Charity Shield, Wembley)

315. Ipswich Town (Portman Road, 11 September 1971)

316. West Ham United

317. Coventry City (2-1 defeat, Filbert Street)

318. 287

319. 29

320. Vancouver Whitecaps

ALAN SMITH

321. 1962

322. Jock Wallace

323. 200: 190 (10)

324. Charlton Athletic

325. 2

326. 76

327. Alvechurch

328. Saudi Arabia

329. Arsenal

330. Striker (Centre forward)

LEICESTER V. WEST BROM

331. 1901 (28 December, at home. WBA won 3-0 and went on to win the title)
332. Allan Clarke
333. Leicester 3, West Bromwich Albion 1
334. Mark Robins
335. 0-0
336. 2-2
337. Mark Grew
338. Frank McLintock
339. Derek Dougan
340. Arthur Rowley

JAMES (JIMMY) WALSH

341. Glasgow
342. Celtic
343. 1957 (v. Fulham, 23 March)
344. Glenavon
345. Wear contact lenses
346. Manchester City (Leicester won 8-4)
347. 1958/1959
348. 1960/1961
349. Fulham (15 December 1962)
350. 1964

PREMIER LEAGUE 2003/2004

351. Paul Dickov
352. Les Ferdinand
353. Craig Hignett
354. Manchester City 0, Leicester City 3

355. Leeds United

356. Tottenham Hotspur 4, Leicester City 4

357. Aston Villa

358. Crewe Alexandra

359. Manchester City (after a 2-2 draw at the COM Stadium and a 3-1 win at the Walkers Stadium)

360. Leeds United and Wolverhampton Wanderers

STEVE LYNEX

361. West Bromwich

362. Birmingham City

363. 1981

364. 5

365. Tottenham Hotspur

366. 5

367. Carlisle United (in a 6-0 win)

368. 1985

369. 1984/1985

370. West Bromwich Albion

STEVE WALSH

371. Wigan Athletic

372. £100,000

373. Bryan Hamilton

374. David Geddis

375. West Bromwich Albion (3-0 win, Filbert Street, 21 October 1987)

376. 1992/1993

377. Blackburn Rovers (Filbert Street, 28 December 1998)

378. 448

379. Norwich City

380. Tony Cottee

PREMIER LEAGUE 1998/1999

381. Manchester United

382. Kasey Keller

383. Chesterfield (Leicester won 2-0 at home and 3-1 away)

384. Tony Cottee

385. Steve Guppy

386. Coventry City (3-0, Filbert Street)

387. Tony Cottee (v. Sunderland)

388. Liverpool

389. Wimbledon

390. 10th

CAPS FOR MY COUNTRY

391.	Tony Cottee (England)	7
392.	Gordon Banks (England)	73
393.	Peter Shilton (England)	125
394.	Frank Worthington (England)	8
395.	Gary McAllister (Scotland)	57
396.	Derek Dougan (Northern Ireland)	43
397.	Muzzy Izzet (Turkey)	8
398.	Gary Lineker (England)	80
399.	Matt Elliott (Scotland)	18
400.	Steve Whitworth (England)	7

MATT GILLIES

401. Loganlea

402. Muirhead

403. **Bolton Wanderers**

404. **Central defender**

405. **1958**

406. **1952 (26 January)**

407. **Allan Clarke from Fulham**

408. **Norman Bullock**

409. **1954/1955**

410. **10 (he handed over to Frank O'Farrell during 1967/1968)**

DIVISION ONE PLAY-OFF WINNERS 1994

411. **4th**

412. **Millwall**

413. **Ian Ormondroyd played 25 games for Derby County**

414. **Tranmere Rovers**

415. **Derby 1, Leicester 0**

416. **Steve Walsh**

417. **Ian Ormondroyd and David Speedie (v. Tranmere Rovers, 2-1, Filbert Street)**

418. **73,802**

419. **6 (4 FA Cup finals and 2 play-off finals)**

420. **Iwan Roberts**

POSITIONS IN THE LEAGUE - 1

421.	2006/2007	The Championship	19th
422.	2004/2005	The Championship	15th
423.	2002/2003	Division One	2nd
424.	2000/2001	Premier League	13th
425.	1998/1999	Premier League	10th
426.	1996/1997	Premier League	9th

427.	1994/1995	Premier League	21st
428.	1992/1993	Division One	6th
429.	1990/1991	Division Two	22nd
430.	1988/1989	Division Two	15th

POT LUCK - 2

431. 6

432. Australia

433. Peterborough United

434. Midfield

435. Bristol Rovers

436. Paul Groves

437. 13

438. Burnley

439. 460: 412 League, 25 FA Cup and 23 League Cup

440. 5

LEAGUE GOALSCORERS - 1

441.	Darren Eadie	2
442.	Marc North	9
443.	Iwan Roberts	41
444.	Dean Smith	1
445.	Mark Robins	12
446.	Peter Welsh	4
447.	Bobby Svarc	2
448.	Muzzy Izzet	38
449.	Steve Lynex	57
450.	Steve Guppy	9

1960s

451. Matt Gillies
452. Kenny Leek (v. Chelsea, 2-2 League draw, Stamford Bridge)
453. Albert Cheeseborough
454. 1968/1969
455. 1962/1963
456. 10 (26 December 1962 to 16 March 1963)
457. Plymouth Argyle
458. Peter Shilton
459. Rodney Fern (v. Manchester United, 17 May 1969)
460. David Tearse

WHO SCORED?

461. James Wesolowski
462. Garry Parker
463. Paul Dickov
464. Craig Hignett
465. Emile Heskey
466. Steve Claridge
467. Julian Joachim
468. Dave Gibson
469. Dennis Bergkamp
470. Ian Marshall

PETER SHILTON

471. Leicester
472. 1966
473. Everton
474. MBE

475. 286
476. Stoke City
477. Nottingham Forest
478. 23
479. True (Against Southampton at The Dell in October 1968)
480. 125

WHO AM I?

481. David Buchanan
482. Martin O'Neill
483. David Gibson
484. Simon Grayson
485. Terry Fenwick
486. Paul Ramsey
487. Steve Thompson
488. Mark Venus
489. Tony Sealy
490. David Webb

GARY MILLS

491. Northampton
492. Notts County
493. Stoke City (1-0 away victory)
494. David Pleat
495. Oxford United
496. 1991/1992 (7 goals)
497. Brian Little
498. 60 (46 League, 2 FA Cup, 4 League Cup, 5 ZDS Cup and 3 play-offs)

499. **Nottingham Forest**

500. **Notts County**

COLIN APPLETON

501. **Scarborough**

502. **1954**

503. **1956 (v. Middlesbrough, away, 29 December)**

504. **1961/1962**

505. **Blackpool (1-1 draw, Filbert Street, 20 August 1960)**

506. **Glenovan (4-1 Leicester away win, 13 September 1961)**

507. **Matt Gillies**

508. **1964/1965 (8 League and 2 League Cup)**

509. **1966**

510. **Charlton Athletic**

LEICESTER CITY V. COVENTRY CITY

511. **1919 (1-0 Leicester win, Filbert Street, 27 September 1919; and then again, 2-1 away from home, a week later)**

512. **Iwan Roberts**

513. **Coventry City 0, Leicester City 2**

514. **Geoff Horsfield**

515. **Muzzy Izzet**

516. **Coventry City 1, Leicester City 8**

517. **Leicester City 5, Coventry City 1**

518. **Frank Worthington**

519. **Tommy English**

520. **Jim Melrose**

RUSSELL OSMAN

521. 1959

522. 1985

523. Everton

524. 8

525. UEFA

526. Gordon Milne

527. True

528. Defender (centre back)

529. Plymouth Argyle

530. Southampton

PREMIER LEAGUE 1999/2000

531. Muzzy Izzet

532. Martin O'Neill

533. True

534. 16

535. Tony Cottee and Phil Gilchrist

536. Emile Heskey

537. False: Leicester won 3-0 at home

538. Tony Cottee

539. Muzzy Izzet

540. Stan Collymore

LEAGUE CUP WINNERS 1964

541. Aldershot, Tranmere Rovers, Gillingham, Norwich City and West Ham United

542. 20

543. Davey Gibson

544. Mike Stringfellow

545. 2 (Dougan and Heath)

546. Frank McLintock

547. 10

548. 17

549. John Sjoberg

550. Gordon Banks

TOP LEAGUE GOALSCORER IN A SEASON

551.	2006/2007	Iain Hume (13)
552.	2005/2006	Iain Hume (9)
553.	2004/2005	David Connolly (13)
554.	2003/2004	Les Ferdinand (12)
555.	2002/2003	Paul Dickov (17)
556.	2001/2002	Brian Deane (6)
557.	2000/2001	Ade Akinbiyi (9)
558.	1999/2000	Tony Cottee (13)
559.	1998/1999	Tony Cottee (10)
560.	1997/1998	Emile Heskey (10)

PREMIER LEAGUE 1994/1995

561. Julian Joachim

562. David Seaman (own goal)

563. Notts County

564. Aston Villa

565. 6

566. Mark Blake

567. Mark Draper

568. David Lowe

569. Watford

570. Steve Walsh

1980s

571. Bristol Rovers
572. Jim Melrose
573. Alan Smith
574. 26
575. Barnsley
576. The Baseball Ground (Derby County FC)
577. Sunderland (2-0 win, Filbert Street; Lineker scored both goals)
578. Alan Smith
579. Swansea City
580. Mike Newell

LEAGUE CUP WINNERS 1997

581. Coca-Cola
582. Scarborough (2-0 and 2-1)
583. Muzzy Izzet
584. Leicester City 2, Manchester United 0
585. Wimbledon (0-0 at home, 1-1 away)
586. Simon Grayson
587. Hillsborough, Sheffield Wednesday FC
588. Ipswich Town (1-0)
589. York City (round 3)
590. Gary Parker

LEN GLOVER

591. Charlton Athletic
592. Outside left (left wing)
593. 50
594. £80,000

595. Arsenal

596. Wolverhampton Wanderers

597. 1973/1974 (12 goals: 9 League, 3 FA Cup)

598. Arsenal

599. Stoke City (1-1 draw)

600. Tampa Bay Rowdies

JOHN SJOBERG

601. Aberdeen

602. 1960

603. Everton

604. 1967/1968

605. He scored two own goals

606. Hull City

607. 19

608. Sheffield United

609. 3 (Matt Gillies, Frank O'Farrell and Jimmy Bloomfield)

610. Rotherham United

DEREK DOUGAN

611. 1939

612. Peterborough United

613. Irish

614. Liverpool

615. True

616. Aston Villa

617. The Doog

618. 43

619. Wolverhampton Wanderers

620. Centre forward

DIVISION TWO CHAMPIONS 1971

621. *1 point (Leicester 59 points, Sheffield United 58 points)*

622. *Portsmouth*

623. *Graham Cross*

624. *Cardiff City*

625. *Ally Brown*

626. *11 (v. Luton, Charlton (twice), Sunderland, Bolton, Watford, Sheffield Wednesday, Swindon, Orient, Carlisle and Bristol City)*

627. *John Farrington (Ally Brown was top goal scorer)*

628. *Birmingham City*

629. *David Nish*

630. *30*

NATIONALITIES - 2

631. *James Chambers*　　　*English*

632. *Hossein Kaebi*　　　*Iranian*

633. *James Wesolowski*　　　*Australian*

634. *Shaun Newton*　　　*English*

635. *Carl Cort*　　　*English*

636. *Martin Fulop*　　　*Hungarian*

637. *Radostin Kishishev*　　　*Bulgarian*

638. *Sergio Hellings*　　　*Dutch*

639. *Stephen Clemence*　　　*English*

640. *Jimmy Nielsen*　　　*Danish*

LEICESTER IN THE LEAGUE CUP

641. *Jimmy Walsh*

642. *Leicester City 4, Stoke City 3*

643. *Leicester City 3, Bristol City 1*

644. *John Farrington (3 goals)*

645. *4th round (1971 and 1976)*

646. *Keith Robson*

647. *1989 (knocked out by Nottingham Forest)*

648. *Bolton Wanderers*

649. *Grimsby Town*

650. *Leeds United (2-1 in 1998/1999 and on penalties in 1999/2000 after a 0-0 draw)*

BIG WINS

651.	*v. Sheffield Wednesday (Away)* *December 2006, Championship*	**4-1**
652.	*v. West Bromwich Albion (Home)* *September 1959, Division One*	**5-0**
653.	*v. Lincoln City (Home)* *December 1955, Division Two*	**4-0**
654.	*v. Sunderland (Home)* *March 2000, Premiership*	**5-2**
655.	*v. Ipswich Town (Home)* *January 1974, Division One*	**5-0**
656.	*v. Rochdale (Away)* *September 1993, Division One*	**6-1**
657.	*v. Sheffield Wednesday (Home)* *January 1987, Division One*	**6-1**
658.	*v. Coventry City (Home)* *December 1984, Division One*	**5-1**
659.	*v. Aston Villa (Home)* *October 1984, Division One*	**5-0**
600.	*v. Fulham (Home)* *August 1952, Division Two*	**6-1**

DIVISION ONE PLAY-OFF WINNERS 1996

661. 5th
662. 4 (Oldham 2-0, Huddersfield 2-1, Birmingham 3-0 and
      Watford 1-0)
663. 0-0
664. Stoke City (2-3 at home and 0-1 away)
665. Iwan Roberts
666. Garry Parker
667. Zeljko Kalac
668. Australian
669. Leicester City 5, Crystal Palace 4 (2-3, Selhurst Park;
      1-0, Filbert Street; 2-1, Wembley)
670. 73,573

STEVE CLARIDGE

671. 1966
672. Crystal Palace
673. Emile Heskey
674. 1996
675. False: he didn't get sent off during the season
676. 17
677. Aston Villa
678. Stan Collymore
679. 12
680. Wolverhampton Wanderers

KEITH WELLER

681. 1971
682. Chelsea
683. Huddersfield Town (Filbert Street, 16 October 1971)

684. Arsenal

685. White tights

686. Ipswich Town

687. Luton Town

688. 1971 (playing for Chelsea)

689. £40,000

690. 58

PAUL RAMSAY

691. Derry

692. 1980/1981

693. 14

694. Oldham Athletic

695. Gordon Milne

696. 1986/1987

697. Wimbledon (Filbert Street, 7 February 1987)

698. West Ham United (3-1 defeat, Upton Park)

699. 308

700. Cardiff City

LEICESTER V. WOLVES

701. Trevor Benjamin

702. Leicester Fosse 2, Wolverhampton Wanderers 0

703. Wolverhampton Wanderers 1, Leicester City 2

704. 1923 (Wolverhampton Wanderers 1, Leicester City 2, 3 March)

705. Wolverhampton Wanderers 4, Leicester City 3

706. Paul Dickov (Leicester won 1-0)

707. 1932

708. Chris Garland

709. Ade Akinbiyi
710. Derek Dougan

DAVID GIBSON

711. Hibernian
712. 1962 (at home to Fulham)
713. Dave Mackay
714. £25,000
715. Wolverhampton Wanderers (Molineaux, 24 March 1962)
716. Mike Stringfellow
717. 1962/1963 (9 League, 3 FA Cup, 1 League Cup)
718. Leeds United (1-1 draw, Filbert Street, 14 September 1968)
719. Aston Villa
720. Exeter City

PREMIER LEAGUE 2000/2001

721. 13th
722. West Ham United
723. Darren Eadie
724. Ipswich Town
725. Muzzy Izzet and Robbie Savage
726. Ade Akinbiyi
727. Gary Rowett
728. 14
729. Matt Jones
730. Tottenham Hotspur

JOHN PATRICK O'NEILL

731. Economic Studies

732. Burnley

733. He is Leicester's most capped player (39 caps)

734. Israel

735. Leeds United

736. 1980/1981

737. Watford (Filbert Street, 13 February 1982)

738. West Ham United (2-0 win, Filbert Street)

739. 1984/1985

740. Queens Park Rangers

LEICESTER V. BIRMINGHAM CITY

741. Leicester City 4, Birmingham 2

742. 1897 (Leicester lost 1-0 at home)

743. 1910 (Leicester won 4-1 away from home)

744. 1945 (Leicester lost 6-2 to the team that went on to win the Football League South title)

745. Steve Claridge

746. Leicester 4, Birmingham 2

747. Leicester 4, Birmingham 2

748. Leicester 0, Birmingham 2

749. They were relegated to Division 3 of the Football League

750. Len Glover

NEIL LENNON

751. 1971

752. Southampton

753. Martin O'Neill

754. Matt Elliott

755. Charlton Athletic

756. 6

757. Midfield

758. Northern Irish

759. Crewe Alexandra

760. Nottingham Forest

LEAGUE APPEARANCES - 1

761. Mark Bright   26 (16)

762. David Kelly   63 (3)

763. Paul Ramsey   278 (12)

764. John Bamber   113

765. Gary Mills   195 (5)

766. John Ridley   17 (7)

767. Graham Cross   596 (3)

768. Peter Shilton   286

769. David Speedie   37

770. Mark Venus   58 (3)

SQUAD NUMBERS 2009/2010

771. Chris Powell   29

772. Bruno Berner   15

773. Andy King   10

774. Robbie Neilson   2

775. Aleksandar Tunchev   5

776. Luke O'Neill   20

777. Jack Hobbs   25

778. Wayne Brown   6

779. Chris Weale   1

780. Matt Oakley   8

LEAGUE CUP WINNERS 2000

781. Martin O'Neill

782. Crystal Palace

783. True

784. Fulham

785. Ian Marshall

786. Matt Elliott

787. False: it was played at Wembley

788. Tim Flowers, Frank Sinclair, Matt Elliott, Gerry Taggart, Robbie Savage, Steve Guppy, Muzzy Izzet, Neil Lennon, Stefan Oakes, Emile Heskey and Tony Cottee

789. Tranmere Rovers

790. Matt Elliott

CITY HONOURS - 1

791. League Cup Winners   2000

792. First Division Play-Off Winners   1996

793. First Division Runners-Up   1929

794. First Division Runners-Up   2003

795. FA Cup Runners-Up   1969

796. League Cup Winners   1964

797. Charity Shield Winners   1971

798. First Division Play-Off Winners   1994

799. FA Cup Runners-Up   1963

800. League Cup Winners   1997

PREMIER LEAGUE 1996/1997

801. Emile Heskey

136

802. *Derby County (Filbert Street, 22 February 1997);*
     Blackburn Rovers (Ewood Park, 11 May 1997)

803. *Ian Marshall (v. Derby County, Filbert Street, 22*
     February 1997)

804. *Middlesbrough 0, Leicester City 2*

805. *Leicester City 2, Newcastle United 0*

806. *Neil Lennon*

807. *Mark Robins*

808. *Steve Claridge*

809. *Simon Grayson*

810. *9th*

POSITIONS IN THE LEAGUE - 2

811.	*1986/1987*	*Division One*	*20th*
812.	*1984/1985*	*Division One*	*15th*
813.	*1982/1983*	*Division Two*	*3rd*
814.	*1980/1981*	*Division One*	*21st*
815.	*1978/1979*	*Division Two*	*17th*
816.	*1976/1977*	*Division One*	*11th*
817.	*1974/1975*	*Division One*	*18th*
818.	*1972/1973*	*Division One*	*16th*
819.	*1970/1971*	*Division Two*	*1st*
820.	*1968/1969*	*Division One*	*21st*

FRANK SINCLAIR

821. *West Bromwich Albion (1991/1992)*

822. *1998*

823. *Derby County (2-1 defeat, Filbert Street, 5 May 1999)*

824. *Lambeth*

825. *Jamaica*

826.   8

827.   Gillingham

828.   3 (v. Coventry, 28 November 1998; v. Liverpool, 19
       September 1999; v. Grimsby, 30 November 2002)

829.   Burnley

830.   Huddersfield

ARTHUR ROWLEY

831.   Wolverhampton

832.   Fulham

833.   1950 (v. Bury, 19 August)

834.   Division Two Championship 1953/1954 and 1956/1957

835.   1956/1957

836.   Fulham

837.   265

838.   West Bromwich Albion (6-2 defeat, The Hawthornes)

839.   Willie Gardiner

840.   Shrewsbury Town

LAWRENCE MAY

841.   1976/1977

842.   Crystal Palace (3-1 defeat, Selhurst Park, 16 December
       1978)

843.   1979/1980

844.   Twice (1979/1980 and 1982/1983)

845.   Frank McLintock

846.   1979/1980

847.   Sutton Coldfield

848.   West Bromwich Albion

849.   Leeds United (2-2 draw, Elland Road, 2 May 1983)

850. Barnsley

PREMIER LEAGUE 2001/2002

851. September

852. Manchester United

853. Micky Adams and Alan Cork

854. 4

855. 12 May 2002

856. 111

857. Derby County 2, Leicester City 3

858. Ipswich Town

859. Leicester City 1, Middlesbrough 2

860. Paul Dickov

LEAGUE GOALSCORERS - 2

861.	Matt Elliott	27
862.	Ricky Hill	0
863.	Ernest Hine	148
864.	Tony Cottee	27
865.	Gary Lineker	95
866.	James Walsh	79
867.	Julian Joachim	25
868.	Dennis Rofe	6
869.	Mike Newell	21
870.	William Hughes	5

LEAGUE APPEARANCES - 2

871.	Gary Lineker	187 (7)
872.	David Nish	228
873.	Alistair Brown	93 (8)

874. Stephen Whitworth   352 (1)

875. Richard Norman   303

876. John Farmer   2

877. James Quinn   13 (18)

878. Alan Smith   190 (10)

879. Howard Riley   193

880. William Cunningham   127

GARY McALLISTER

881. Motherwell

882. 1985

883. Oxford United (4-4 draw, Filbert Street, 2 October 1985)

884. 1989/1990 (10 goals)

885. 3

886. Alan Smith (19 goals)

887. 47

888. 1990

889. Leeds United (2-1 defeat, Elland Road, 28 November 1990)

890. Leeds United

LEICESTER V. DERBY COUNTY

891. Derby County 2, Leicester City 0 (2 November 1996)

892. Leicester Fosse 6, Derby County 0 (26 February 1910)

893. 0-0 draw (Filbert Street, 19 April 1975)

894. Leicester City 2, Derby County 2

895. 1-0

896. Dean Sturridge

897. Leicester City 3, Derby County 1

898. *Trevor Benjamin*

899. *Garry Rowett*

900. *Matty Fryatt*

JULIAN JOACHIM

901. *1974*

902. *Barnsley*

903. *25*

904. *Brian Little*

905. *Tottenham Hotspur*

906. *Steve Agnew and Steve Walsh (2)*

907. *Aston Villa*

908. *Sunderland*

909. *Ian Ormondroyd and Iwan Roberts*

910. *Darlington*

MIKE STRINGFELLOW

911. *Kirby in Ashfield*

912. *The Thin Man*

913. *He referred to Mike as 'my secret weapon'*

914. *£25,000*

915. *Mansfield*

916. *Everton*

917. *Fulham*

918. *14 (1961/1962 to 1974/1975)*

919. *97*

920. *1967/1968 (14 League and Cup goals)*

HAT-TRICK HEROES

921. *Stan Collymore*

922. Arthur Rowley

923. Gary Lineker

924. Alan Smith

925. David Connolly

926. Iwan Roberts

927. David Kelly (Mick Quinn scored a hat-trick for
Newcastle)

928. Steve Moran

929. Gary Lineker

930. Jim Melrose

NIGEL PEARSON

931. Graham

932. 2008

933. True

934. MK Dons

935. Defender

936. True: during August 2008

937. Carlisle United

938. Ian Holloway

939. 1963

940. False: Nigel never played for Leicester City during his
playing days

POT LUCK - 3

941. 6

942. David Pleat

943. Left back

944. Grimsby Town

945. Newcastle United

946. Striker

947. Ally Brown

948. Frank Sinclair

949. Hull City

950. Right back

LEAGUE ONE CHAMPIONS - 2008/2009

951. 27

952. Peterborough United

953. Leeds United

954. True: won 4 and drew 1

955. Leyton Orient

956. Lloyd Dyer

957. Chris Powell

958. 27

959. Nigel Pearson

960. Crewe Alexandra

BOBBY ROBERTS

961. Motherwell

962. 1963 (v. Fulham, 21 September)

963. £41,000

964. Frank McLintock

965. Everton

966. 1964/1965 (12 goals in all competitions)

967. Oxford United

968. 36

969. 1966/1967

970. Mansfield Town

CITY HONOURS - 2

971.	Second Division Champions	1980
972.	First Division Play-Off Runners-Up	2003
973.	Second Division Champions	1971
974.	FA Cup Runners-Up	1961
975.	Second Division Champions	1957
976.	League Cup Runners-Up	1999
977.	Second Division Champions	1937
978.	FA Cup Runners-Up	1949
979.	Second Division Champions	1954
980.	Second Division Champions	1925

GRAHAM CROSS

981. 60

982. Birmingham City (29 April 1961)

983. 1962/1963 (8 League and Cup goals)

984. 5

985. 37

986. 1969/1970 and 1970/1971

987. 1975/1976

988. Brighton and Hove Albion

989. Preston North End

990. Lincoln City

WHERE DID THEY GO? - 2

991.	Spencer Prior	Derby County
992.	Momo Sylla	Kilmarnock
993.	David Rennie	Leeds United
994.	Tony Spearing	Plymouth Argyle
995.	Andy Johnson	Barnsley

996. *Nicky Cross* — *Port Vale*

997. *Frank Sinclair* — *Burnley*

998. *Patrick McCarthy* — *Charlton Athletic*

999. *Arnar Gunnlaugsson* — *Dundee United*

1000. *Mark Venus* — *Wolverhampton Wanderers*

NOTES

NOTES

NOTES

NOTES

OTHER BOOKS BY CHRIS COWLIN:

* Celebrities' Favourite Football Teams

* The British TV Sitcom Quiz Book

* The Cricket Quiz Book

* The Gooners Quiz Book

* The Horror Film Quiz Book

* The Official Aston Villa Quiz Book

* The Official Birmingham City Quiz Book

* The Official Brentford Quiz Book

* The Official Bristol Rovers Quiz Book

* The Official Burnley Quiz Book

* The Official Bury Quiz Book

* The Official Carlisle United Quiz Book

* The Official Carry On Quiz Book

* The Official Chesterfield Football Club Quiz Book

* The Official Colchester United Quiz Book

* The Official Coventry City Quiz Book

* The Official Doncaster Rovers Quiz Book

* The Official Greenock Morton Quiz Book

* The Official Heart of Midlothian Quiz Book

* The Official Hereford United Quiz Book

* The Official Hull City Quiz Book

OTHER BOOKS BY CHRIS COWLIN:

* The Official Leicester City Quiz Book

* The Official Macclesfield Town Quiz Book

* The Official Norwich City Football Club Quiz

* The Official Notts County Quiz Book

* The Official Peterborough United Quiz Book

* The Official Port Vale Quiz Book

* The Official Rochdale AFC Quiz Book

* The Official Rotherham United Quiz Book

* The Official Sheffield United Quiz Book

* The Official Shrewsbury Town Quiz Book

* The Official Stockport County Quiz Book

* The Official Watford Football Club Quiz Book

* The Official West Bromwich Albion Quiz Book

* The Official Wolves Quiz Book

* The Official Yeovil Town Quiz Book

* The Reality Television Quiz Book

* The Southend United Quiz Book

* The Sunderland AFC Quiz Book

* The Ultimate Derby County Quiz Book

* The West Ham United Quiz Book

www.apexpublishing.co.uk